No matter how small, every moment can be transformed into something extraordinary with food, creativity, and love. Whether you're sharing a table with friends and family or savoring quiet time alone, each dish celebrates the beauty in everyday life. Mother-and-daughter duo Trudy Crane and Chloé Crane-Leroux believe romanticizing your life means living close to your true self and finding a flutter of excitement in the mundane. This approach has stayed consistent throughout their lives—from Trudy raising her daughter in Montreal's vibrant culture to Chloé's adult life in New York City and their frequent travels to Europe together.

The Artful Way to Plant-Based Cooking showcases the joy of crafting a meal that nourishes your body. With a collection of more than eighty good-for-you recipes, this cookbook offers many dishes that will please longtime vegans and people curious about plant-based cooking, and provides lists of the essentials you need in your pantry to gain the health benefits of this way of eating.

Cooking with fresh, local ingredients is a way of life in European countries. That's where the authors found inspiration to write this book: in the richness of the food, the beauty of the architecture, and the wonder of luscious landscapes—beautifully photographed by Chloé in Spain and France. Influences shine in appetizers such as Vibrant Beet and Pistachio Hummus; date-night dishes like Pappardelle Mushroom Bolognese; main dishes such as Ricotta and Squash Galette, perfect for entertaining; and, of course, desserts like Strawberry and Cream Cake and Decadent Double Dark Chocolate Cookies—all of which are so flavorful you'll forget they're even plant-based.

Embark on a culinary journey with two romantics whose recipes and exquisite styling redefine everyday beauty in the heart of a home—the kitchen.

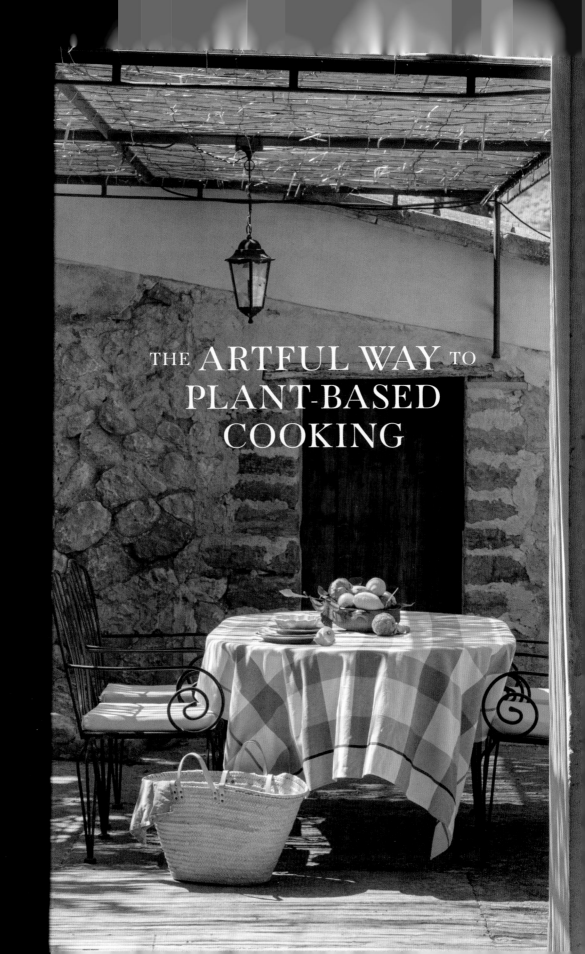

THE **ARTFUL WAY** TO **PLANT-BASED COOKING**

THE ARTFUL WAY TO PLANT-BASED COOKING

NOURISHING RECIPES AND HEARTFELT MOMENTS

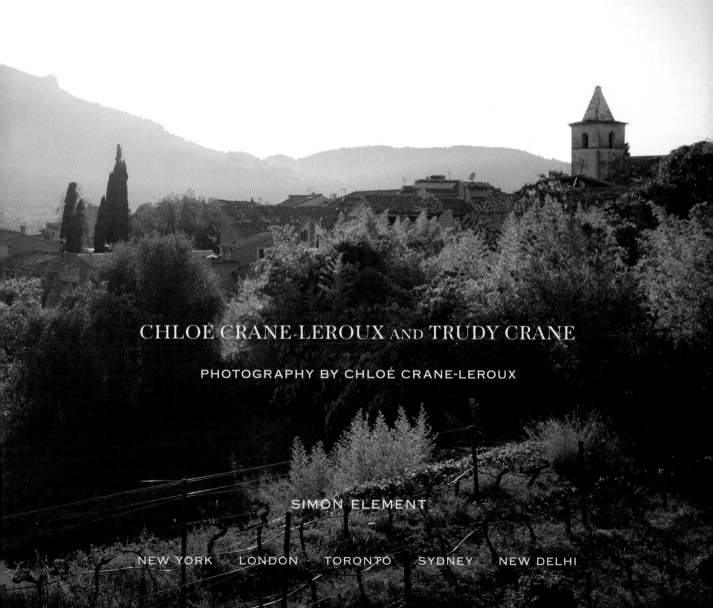

CHLOÉ CRANE-LEROUX AND TRUDY CRANE

PHOTOGRAPHY BY CHLOÉ CRANE-LEROUX

SIMON ELEMENT

NEW YORK   LONDON   TORONTO   SYDNEY   NEW DELHI

SIMON
ELEMENT

An Imprint of Simon & Schuster, LLC
1230 Avenue of the Americas New York, NY 10020

First Simon Element hardcover edition September 2024

SIMON ELEMENT and colophon are trademarks of Simon & Schuster, LLC

Simon & Schuster: Celebrating 100 Years of Publishing in 2024

For information about special discounts for bulk purchases,
please contact Simon & Schuster Special Sales at 1-866-506-1949
or business@simonandschuster.com.

The Simon & Schuster Speakers Bureau can bring authors to your live event.
For more information or to book an event, contact the Simon & Schuster Speakers Bureau
at 1-866-248-3049 or visit our website at www.simonspeakers.com.

Interior design by Natasshia Neary
Prop styling by Trudy Crane
Food styling by Sappho Hatzis
Photo inside back endpaper by Javi Dardo
Photos pages x, 4, 192, 232, 268 by Carlota Grau

Manufactured in China

10 9 8 7 6 5 4 3 2 1

Library of Congress Control Number: 2024934966

ISBN 978-1-6680-2694-6
ISBN 978-1-6680-2695-3 (ebook)

This book is dedicated to all the exceptional moments,
both inside and outside the kitchen, when love, laughter,
and shared experiences have nourished our lives.

CONTENTS

ACKNOWLEDGMENTS

We would like to express our heartfelt gratitude to the following individuals and organizations who played a significant role in the creation of this book. Your contributions have been invaluable, and we are deeply humbled by your support.

To my beautiful, talented, and inspirational daughter, Chloé: Thank you for giving me the strength to face any challenge and persevere through difficult moments. Your attention to detail and ability to find beauty in everything you do truly touches my heart. I love you more than words can express, and I am incredibly proud of the person you are and the person you strive to become. —Trudy

To the best mother any daughter could have: I adore you. Your endless determination and support throughout this process was incredible. I couldn't have done it without you. You inspire me every day and I feel so deeply thankful to be able to do this by your side. You will forever be my favorite person to work, travel, and create with. —Chloé

To my online community, whose support has allowed me to pursue my dreams: Over the past few years, your encouragement, messages, and active engagement with my work has made me grow and be creative in a way I never thought possible. I am eternally thankful for each and every one of you. —Chloé

To our amazing editor, Justin Schwartz: From the moment we met you, we knew you were the one! Your enthusiasm and conviction about the book's potential matched our own, and we so appreciate your patience and support throughout this process. We are truly grateful to have you by our side and can't thank you enough.

To the entire team at Simon Element and Simon and Schuster: Thank you for your commitment and meticulous efforts in bringing this book to life.

A special thank-you to our literary agent, Kim Lindman: Your clear direction and unwavering support kept us motivated and encouraged throughout this journey. Your belief in our vision meant the world to us, and we are grateful for your guidance every step of the way.

Thank you so much to Sappho Hatzis, for your invaluable help and support in creating this book. Your dedication during our trip to Spain, cooking and styling countless recipes, was truly remarkable, and your talent and energy throughout the entire process were truly inspiring.

We give our heartfelt thanks to Natasshia Neary for your incredible vision in designing our book. Your attention to detail and sensitivity shines through in every page, and we are in awe of your talent and dedication. You truly brought our recipes and photos to life, capturing the essence of what we wanted to convey about food, beauty, and living an artful life.

To my beautiful sister, Nancy, thank you for your unwavering love and support. Writing portions of the book at Gabriola Island was the peaceful haven I needed, and your presence and guidance were invaluable. I appreciate your dedication in reading every page and providing insightful advice. I love you with all my heart. —Trudy

My darling Robert, you have been my greatest source of support throughout the two year-long process of creating this book. I am immensely grateful for your patience and understanding. You are the partner I had been waiting for all my life, and I feel blessed to have you by my side. —Trudy

To my partner in love and life, Clément, thank you for always believing in me and pushing me to be the best version of myself. Your belief in my culinary vision and your willingness to taste-test countless iterations have been instrumental in bringing these recipes to life. Thank you for being my confidant, my sous-chef, and my biggest cheerleader. You enrich my life in every way. —Chloé

To Mauricio Padilla from Hinter Company, Natalia Swarz from Hotel Weekend, and Pablo Rovira from Via Emporda, we are so grateful for all of you to have made our trip to La Higuera in Spain an absolutely magical experience. We couldn't have dreamt of a more idyllic place to have ended the shoot of the book.

To Catherine at Château Marcellus in France, we can't thank you enough for graciously allowing us to stay at your incredible property. Your generosity and kindness during our visit went above and beyond, and we are immensely grateful for the experience.

To Can Quatre, our stay at your magnificent family-run hotel in Mallorca was a constant source of inspiration during our photo shoot. We are deeply thankful for the opportunity to have called it our home during that time.

Thank you to Anthony from Zio and Sons for letting us shoot in the "Old Hudson" apartments. The perfect spot to finish up the last few recipes in the book.

Special thanks to Anthropologie and DÔEN for providing us with some of the beautiful clothes used in our photo shoot. Your contributions added an extra touch of elegance and style to our work.

INTRODUCTION

When we embarked on writing this cookbook, we delved deep into the food culture that shaped us. We thought not only about the recipes we wanted to share but also about the stories and experiences that influenced our journey. Our book reflects this blend of our passions, creativity, and shared memories. It is an invitation to others to discover the joy of savoring beautiful moments around the table, to infuse their own lives with art, and to enjoy the simple pleasures of delicious food and meaningful connections.

For us a perfect example of this was during our trip to Spain to shoot the photos of the recipes for this book. We took an evening at the end of our trip to explore the seaside town of Calella de Palafrugell in the Catalonia region. We had originally planned to dine at a restaurant opening at 8:00 p.m., but exhaustion led us to a smaller restaurant that opened an hour earlier. Arriving at an unusually early dining hour in Spain, we were the only customers in the restaurant. The decor of the restaurant was incredibly simple with a white-tiled interior, concrete counters, and tin plates for serving. We opted to share five vegetable dishes and were completely enchanted with the delicious food and fresh flavors of each dish. After dark, we walked to our car while watching the sea crash against the cliffs. The beauty of the place, food, and people moved us to tears as we realized that these are the simple moments we yearn for and seek in our everyday lives, both in our cooking and at our table.

Our shared love of travel has always been a deeply meaningful connection between us as mother and daughter. Exploring Europe, with its diverse culinary traditions and captivating landscapes, has been a source of profound joy. It felt only natural to capture those moments in our book. That journey was a voyage of pure love, one that still brings up emotions as we reminisce over each photograph. It brought us laughter and tears, often simultaneously.

Arriving in Mallorca, we made the decision to rent a larger car to accommodate our numerous bags. The bags were filled with essentials, from vegan cheeses and butter to linens, aprons, dishes, and, of course, clothing. What we hadn't anticipated was the narrowness of the streets, on which our car barely fit. On one side, there was a sheer cliff, and on the other, a towering mountain, with small cars lining the road. Chloé jumped out of the car and took on the role of guiding us through the streets, inching us along and avoiding any mishaps. After a few tears, we couldn't help but laugh at the absurdity of it all. Finally we reached our destination, perched high on a mountain, and took a moment to catch our breath. The scent of nearby olive groves, sheep meandering into and out of view, and the breathtaking valley below bathed in soft, ever-present dust-filtered light left us in awe. We hugged and shared a laugh.

Cooking with fresh, local ingredients has always been an important consideration for us. Whether it's the flavor of ripe tomatoes or the sweet succulence of strawberries, such experiences take on a sensory richness of their own. This depth of flavor is central to our approach to crafting plant-based meals. We draw inspiration from the culinary traditions of the countries we explore, infusing their influences into our recipes, our dining table, and our daily lives. Whether we are in our kitchens at home in Montreal and New York or reflecting on our travels, this practice keeps our spirits wandering the world throughout the year.

NURTURING MEANINGFUL TRADITIONS

TRUDY WRITES: Many people are curious about our close mother-daughter bond. The truth is that our relationship is unique and has been since Chloé was a little girl. From a very early age, it was clear that we viewed the world through the same artistic lens. We had our own little universe where we sought beauty in everything we encountered. Our conversations were filled with discussions about art, home decor, flowers—anything and everything that ignited our creative senses. Even as a child, Chloé actively engaged in these discussions, her curiosity shining through as she asked questions and shared her own unique perspective.

To encourage her creativity, I gave her a camera when she was just three years old. I was working in fashion marketing at the time, and she attended many of my photo shoots. She would watch the photographer and models intently. At the age of thirteen, she announced to me that she wanted to be a photographer, and from that day forward she carried a camera with her everywhere. She never changed her mind and never wavered from her goal. Her love of capturing beauty was born, and she has not stopped developing her art since then.

Originally from western Canada, I moved to Montreal, Quebec, in my midtwenties. The charm of the city immediately captivated me, particularly the ritual of sitting at the table for hours, indulging in good food, engaging in lively conversations, savoring wine, and immersing myself in the French language that was spoken around me. It was an entirely new experience, as I hadn't grown up with such traditions, but it felt incredibly natural.

Chloé was born a few years later and grew up in Montreal's vibrant culture. Her first language is French, but she learned English early on, and we spoke a mix of the two languages in our home. As she grew up, we traveled very often to France and throughout Europe. Those trips made us both love and appreciate the focus on fresh food and ingredients. Between visiting museums, we would try a variety of delicious bites at various restaurants or make fresh food at our apartment rental.

Our lives revolved around treasured moments, often centered around food. Every mealtime was an opportunity to make it special. Whether it was our family suppers on weekdays, where we set the table, lit a candle, and shared stories of our day, or our cherished apéro before dinner, the intentional pause of that moment allowed us to be present, grateful, and deeply connected.

Our dinner gatherings often expanded to include friends and family. We sought any excuse to host, whether celebrating a birthday, moving into a new home, or simply embracing the arrival of the weekend. Each gathering transformed into a joyful party, where both kids and adults danced to the latest pop tunes, eventually transitioning to French music for the final hour of the evening.

ROMANTICIZING YOUR LIFE

As a ceramic artist, my journey in creating tableware spans more than a decade. It was a significant turning point in my life when I decided to fully embrace the artistic path after spending more than thirty years in the world of fashion marketing. Deep down, I had always yearned for a career that would bring me closer to my true self. It is why I always encouraged Chloé to pursue her own passions and find happiness in her chosen path.

Society often pressures us to choose the safe route, but I have always believed that when you do what you love, success will naturally follow. So I took the leap, leaving behind my lucrative corporate job to embark on that journey. The initial years were not easy, but I was determined to make a change that would align with the things I hold dear: food, art, and beauty.

Around the same time, Chloé left Montreal to study at Parsons School of Design in New York, with dreams of becoming a fashion photographer. It seemed like a natural progression after years of accompanying me to countless photo shoots. However, as she went deeper into her studies and professional work, she had an epiphany: fashion photography wasn't her true calling. Our lives had always revolved around the table, and it was through capturing food stories that she discovered her genuine passion: food photography. In that moment, our career paths intertwined, driven by our shared vision of making the art of the table the centerpiece of our lives.

So what does it mean to romanticize your life? For us it is living close to our true selves. It's the quest to find the transformative moments that give us a flutter of excitement, whether through crafting a beautiful ceramic dish from discarded clay or finding the perfect fallen branch to adorn a vase. For Chloé, it's through capturing the play of sunlight streaming into a dimly lit room or hosting an intimate gathering for her friends in her home. Sometimes it's as simple as wearing a beautiful dress to uplift our spirits. These are the moments that touch our hearts.

EMBRACING A PLANT-BASED LIFESTYLE

Embracing a plant-based lifestyle was not an early decision for either of us. When Chloé left home for university, she quickly transitioned to plant-based eating, and I followed suit soon after. Initially, we navigated through different phases, trying to understand the best approach to plant-based eating. We watched YouTube videos, consumed an abundance of bananas, and struggled to create interesting and nutritious meals. However, Chloé's collaborations with chefs and food stylists during her photography work provided invaluable insights. She realized that the same techniques used to spice meat and chicken could be applied to tofu and other plant-based ingredients. She began experimenting with flavorful combinations that resulted in fresh, delicious, straightforward dishes. Our recipes reflect this approach: versatile, easy to make, and featuring ingredients that can be swapped or substituted according to personal preferences and seasonal availability.

Our cookbook features primarily recipes emphasizing the importance of eating seasonally, using fresh, locally sourced ingredients. While shooting the recipe photos in Spain, I would visit the morning markets in Palma de Mallorca or Girona to select the ingredients for the day's shoot. Occasionally, a particular vegetable would be out of season, forcing us to improvise and adapt the recipe to what was readily available. We embraced that flexibility, recognizing that the same recipe could be transformed with different vegetables according to the season—for example, by using asparagus in spring and broccoli later in the year.

In addition to making the recipes in this book, hopefully you will view it as a source of inspiration. We show you how plant-based meals can be delicious and satisfying, even if enjoyed occasionally. We encourage you to create beautiful table settings, even when dining alone. We hope to inspire you to travel, pursue your passions, and forge deeper connections with your loved ones. Moreover, we encourage you to be mindful of your surroundings and seek out the moments that touch your heart. These may include lighting a candle and savoring a meal prepared with love, or creating your own rituals that mark special occasions and forge lasting memories. Ultimately, we hope this book inspires you to find joy in the art of living beautifully, one meal at a time.

BUILDING A NOURISHING VEGAN KITCHEN

CHLOÉ WRITES: Both my mom and I acknowledge that we are not perfect vegans. Though we strive to avoid consuming or using any animal products, we sometimes fall short of that goal. However, we firmly believe in the importance of transitioning toward a plant-based diet for several reasons. First, our love of animals drives us to minimize their suffering as much as possible. Second, we have personally witnessed the incredible health benefits that come with a well-planned plant-based lifestyle. And last, we recognize the positive impact it can have on the planet.

Rather than engaging in the statistics, politics, and debates surrounding veganism, we prefer to focus on encouraging those around us. Our aim is to inspire others to start by making small changes, whether that means following a plant-based diet once a week or incorporating plant-based dinners into their routine. We understand that everyone's journey is unique and making changes can be challenging.

Transitioning to a plant-based diet doesn't have to be overwhelming or abrupt. It can be a gradual process, just as it was for us. For Trudy, it involved letting go of meat first, then fish, followed by cheese, and finally eggs. It took nearly a year to fully transition. I, on the other hand, became vegetarian before adopting a vegan lifestyle. Each person's path is unique and personal.

By sharing our experiences and insights, we hope to empower others embarking on their plant-based journey. Our goal is to provide guidance and support, particularly during those initial stages, when having a well-stocked pantry can make all the difference. So spice up your meals, explore new flavors, and enjoy the transformative power of plant-based cooking. Remember, every step counts, and you are making a difference every day by exploring new ways to cook delicious, healthy plant-based recipes.

Ensuring that your pantry is stocked with the essentials is a key step in transitioning to a plant-based diet. Chances are, you already have many of these items tucked away in your fridge and pantry! As you gradually incorporate the remaining ingredients, you'll discover just how effortlessly you can create the mouthwatering recipes featured in this book.

VEGGIES

avocados

beets (canned are fine)

broccoli or broccolini

butternut squash or sweet potato

cauliflower

garlic

mushrooms

peas (frozen)

scallions

shallots

tomatoes

white or red onions

FRESH & DRIED FRUITS

blueberries

dried cranberries

dried figs

lemons

strawberries or raspberries

FRIDGE STAPLES

firm or extra-firm tofu

plant-based milk, such as oat or almond

vegan butter

vegan mayonnaise

vegan puff pastry (store in the freezer)

vegan unsweetened plain yogurt

FLOURS

all-purpose

almond

chickpea

VEGAN CHEESES

feta

parmesan

ricotta or spreadable cheese

shredded mozzarella

SPICES & SAUCES

baking powder

baking soda

cumin

Dijon mustard

flaky sea salt

garlic powder

herbes de Provence

hot sauce

Italian seasoning

kosher salt

maple syrup

nutritional yeast

onion powder

oregano

paprika

peppercorns

soy sauce

sumac

thyme

tahini

vegetable broth

GRAINS & RICE

basmati rice

couscous

farro

oats

quinoa

NUTS, SEEDS & LEGUMES

almonds

cashews (raw)

chia seeds

chickpeas (canned)

flaxseed meal (ground flaxseed)

lentils (dried or canned)

pecans

pumpkin seeds

sesame seeds

walnuts

NUT BUTTERS

almond butter

peanut butter

OILS, FATS & VINEGARS

avocado oil or neutral-flavored oil

balsamic vinegar

coconut milk (unsweetened)

coconut oil

extra-virgin olive oil

SWEETENERS

coconut sugar

maple syrup

APÉRO

CHLOÉ WRITES: The apéro holds a special place in our hearts as our favorite time of the day. Whether we find ourselves peacefully alone or in the company of others, we both make it a ritual to carve out time for an apéro almost every day. It's those simple moments that bring so much joy, whether a humble pairing of flatbread and wine or a flavorful beet hummus with rustic herb and seed crackers. For us, the true beauty of the apéro lies in the time it gives us to create connections, whether alone or with our partners or friends who join us. It acts as a much-needed pause between work and dinner, a moment of reflection on the day.

When we have the pleasure of sharing the apéro with a group of friends, it always becomes a singular experience. Picture the scene: soft cushions scattered on the floor, an intimate gathering around the coffee table, and an abundant spread of delicious small bites prepared with love. In these magical moments, time seems to stand still as we immerse ourselves in deep conversations, hearty laughter, and the joy of being together. It's these gatherings that often flow seamlessly into late-night suppers, where warmth and camaraderie take precedence over formality and we take pure pleasure in one another's company.

PROVENÇAL CHICKPEA FLATBREAD

SERVES 4 · PREP TIME: 35 MINUTES · COOK TIME: 12 TO 15 MINUTES

1 cup (250 mL) chickpea flour

1 tablespoon (15 mL) flaxseed meal

1 tablespoon (15 mL) nutritional yeast

½ teaspoon (2.5 mL) kosher salt

2 tablespoons (30 mL) extra-virgin olive oil, divided

2 tablespoons (30 mL) za'atar, for garnish

CHLOÉ WRITES: When I was a kid and we visited the French Riviera, one of my favorite things was exploring the local markets. I'd stand there, absolutely fascinated, as talented vendors worked their magic, making socca, a flatbread, on hot griddles. The anticipation would build as I eagerly waited for my turn to taste that irresistible treat. Those precious moments of devouring socca are forever etched in my memory, reminding me of the incredible sense of discovery, the beauty of keeping things simple, and the amazing ability of food to evoke emotions and create lasting bonds. Now, whenever I re-create those flavors in my own kitchen, it's like a joyful journey back to the vibrant markets and sunny beaches of the Mediterranean.

Preheat the oven to 400°F (200°C) and place a medium cast-iron skillet on the middle rack (you can use any ovenproof frying pan or skillet).

In a medium bowl, whisk together the chickpea flour, flaxseed meal, nutritional yeast, and salt. Make a little well in the middle and add 1 tablespoon (15 mL) olive oil and 1 cup (250 mL) water and whisk together. Once combined, let the batter rest for at least 30 minutes.

About 15 minutes before you are ready to bake the flatbread, carefully remove the hot skillet from the oven and coat the bottom with the remaining 1 tablespoon (15 mL) olive oil. Pour the batter into the middle of the skillet and allow it to spread naturally.

Return the skillet to the oven and cook for 5 minutes, then change the setting to broil and cook for an additional 5 to 7 minutes, until the top is golden brown.

Remove from the oven and sprinkle with the za'atar. Cut into 8 slices and enjoy while warm.

MEDITERRANEAN SPINACH PIES

MAKES 12 • PREP TIME: 15 MINUTES • COOK TIME: 20 MINUTES

8 vegan phyllo sheets

6 cups (1.5 L) packed fresh spinach, roughly chopped

1 cup (250 mL) diced red onion

1½ cups (375 mL) spreadable vegan cheese (chive and herbs preferred)

1 teaspoon (5 mL) kosher salt

2 teaspoons (10 mL) freshly ground black pepper

2 tablespoons (30 mL) freshly squeezed lemon juice

3 garlic cloves, minced

2 cups (500 mL) vegan butter, melted

1 tablespoon (15 mL) sesame seeds

CHLOÉ SAYS: For as long as I can remember, the mouthwatering scent of phyllo dough and the irresistible combination of spinach and vegan cheese has been a mainstay in my kitchen. Also known as spanakopita, a beloved traditional Greek recipe, these pies have become a staple at apéro time. It's the kind of dish that makes our friends gather around, unable to resist its golden, flaky goodness and flavorful filling. You'll find yourself grabbing another after you just finished one.

Two hours before making the spinach pies, take the phyllo dough from the freezer, place in the bottom of the fridge, and let thaw in its packaging.

Preheat the oven to 400°F (200°C), place a rack in the middle position, and line 2 medium rimmed baking sheets with parchment paper.

In a large bowl, combine the spinach, onion, vegan cheese, salt, pepper, lemon juice, and garlic and mix well. Set aside.

Open the phyllo box and cover the phyllo sheets with a damp kitchen towel. Take 1 phyllo sheet and place on a cutting board or clean surface. Brush all over with vegan butter, then top with another sheet of phyllo. Brush the second sheet of phyllo with vegan butter, then slice the sheets into three long vertical strips.

Place 2 tablespoons of the filling at the top corner on a phyllo strip. Fold the corner over the filling to create the beginning of a triangle, then continue folding until you have reached the bottom of the strip. Place the triangle on the prepared baking sheet. Repeat steps 4 and 5 with the remaining filling and phyllo sheets.

Brush the triangles with more vegan butter and sprinkle with the sesame seeds. Bake for 15 to 20 minutes, until golden and crisp.

Let cool slightly and serve warm.

VIBRANT BEET AND PISTACHIO HUMMUS

6 small beets

one 15.5-ounce (439 g) can chickpeas, strained
(reserve the liquid for Tofu Schnitzel with Coleslaw,
page 56, or Crumbed Artichokes, page 43)

⅓ cup (80 mL) tahini

juice of 1 lemon

½ cup (125 mL) avocado oil

3 to 4 garlic cloves

kosher salt and freshly ground black pepper

3 ice cubes (optional)

TOPPINGS

roughly chopped pistachios

white sesame seeds

roughly chopped white onion

vegan feta

extra-virgin olive oil

roughly chopped fresh dill

kosher salt

Grab your apron and create a vibrant twist on the classic dip. This hummus is perfect for an apéro and a great base for any dish. Smear it on your plate and top with roasted veggies, and you have a perfect easy lunch or dinner. You can reserve the chickpea liquid, called aquafaba, for another use.

Cut the stems off the beets and discard, then poke holes in the beets with a fork. Place the beets in a medium pot with water to cover by 2 inches and bring to a boil. Reduce the heat and simmer until the beets are fork tender, 25 to 30 minutes. Drain and, when cool enough to handle, remove the skins and dice the beets.

To a food processor or blender, add the beets, chickpeas, tahini, lemon juice, avocado oil, and garlic, season with salt and pepper to taste, and blend until smooth. For a thicker hummus, add the ice cubes.

Transfer the hummus to a large decorative bowl and serve with the toppings alongside. Enjoy with your favorite crusty bread, crackers, crudités, or flatbread (see page 25).

SPICY ROASTED SWEET POTATO BOUCHÉES WITH COCONUT SOUR CREAM

SERVES 4 TO 6 • PREP TIME: 10 MINUTES • COOK TIME: 25 MINUTES

4 small sweet potatoes, skin on,
    washed and halved or quartered lengthwise

2 tablespoons (30 mL) extra-virgin olive oil

¼ teaspoon (1.25 mL) paprika,
    plus more for garnish

¼ teaspoon (1.25 mL) cayenne pepper

kosher salt and freshly ground black pepper

1 cup (250 mL) unsweetened plain vegan
    coconut yogurt

2 tablespoons (30 mL) freshly squeezed lime juice

⅓ cup (80 mL) sliced scallions, for garnish

2 tablespoons (30 mL) chopped fresh chives,
    for garnish

These bouchées are the perfect small apéro bites, or dinner appetizers. With just a handful of simple ingredients and minimal preparation, you can have them ready in no time. All you need to do is roast the sweet potatoes with a sprinkle of spices, whip up the creamy coconut sour cream, and assemble them. Whether you're hosting a gathering or simply craving a flavorful snack, this recipe ensures that you can impress your guests or enjoy a small meal without spending hours in the kitchen.

Preheat the oven to 400°F (200°C) and place a rack in the middle position.

On a parchment paper–lined baking pan, coat the sweet potatoes with the olive oil and season with the paprika, cayenne pepper, and salt and pepper. Place in the oven and roast for 20 to 25 minutes, until fork tender.

In a small bowl, combine the coconut yogurt and lime juice. Mix well.

Once the sweet potatoes are cooked, serve with a dollop of the coconut yogurt-lime mixture, topped with the scallions and chives, and a sprinkling of paprika.

SPICY CRISPY CHICKPEAS

SERVES 4 TO 6 • PREP TIME: 5 MINUTES • COOK TIME: 35 MINUTES

one 15.5-ounce (439 g) can chickpeas, strained (reserve the liquid for Tofu Schnitzel with Coleslaw, page 56, or Crumbed Artichokes, page 43) and rinsed

¼ teaspoon (1.25 mL) extra-virgin olive oil

½ teaspoon (2.5 mL) kosher salt, plus more to taste

freshly ground black pepper

¼ teaspoon (1.25 mL) smoked paprika

½ teaspoon (2.5 mL) ground cumin

½ teaspoon (2.5 mL) nutritional yeast

With their convenient bite-size form, these spiced chickpeas are the ultimate on-the-go snack. Pack them in a resealable bag or container, and you'll have a satisfying pick-me-up whenever you need it. They're also a fantastic addition to any apéro platter, offering a spicy and crunchy alternative to traditional nibbles.

Preheat the oven to 375°F (190°C) and line a baking pan with parchment paper.

Dry the chickpeas as much as possible, letting them sit on a paper towel–lined pan for at least 15 minutes.

In a medium bowl, toss the chickpeas with the olive oil, ½ teaspoon (2.5 mL) salt, and a few grinds of pepper. Roast in the oven on the prepared pan for 20 minutes, tossing them halfway through cooking.

Remove the chickpeas from the oven, sprinkle with the smoked paprika and cumin, and toss to combine. Return the pan to the oven for another 15 to 20 minutes, until they are super crispy but not overdone.

Remove from the oven and season with the nutritional yeast and more salt to taste. Let cool and serve at room temperature.

BEET CARPACCIO WITH ROASTED CARROT AND PINE NUT PESTO

SERVES 4 • PREP TIME: 10 MINUTES • COOK TIME: 20 MINUTES

4 canned or fresh cooked whole beets
    (see page 29 for Beet Hummus
    on how to cook beets)

FOR THE PESTO

4 medium carrots, peeled and cut into 1-inch lengths

kosher salt and freshly ground black pepper

2 tablespoons (30 mL) plus ¾ cup (180 mL)
    extra-virgin olive oil, plus more for drizzle

2 cups (500 mL) firmly packed basil leaves

2 garlic cloves, finely chopped

2 tablespoons (30 mL) freshly squeezed lemon juice

½ teaspoon (2.5 mL) salt

⅓ cup (80 mL) toasted pine nuts

⅓ cup (80 mL) toasted unsalted walnuts

4 teaspoons (20 mL) nutritional yeast

1 teaspoon (5 mL) freshly ground black pepper

⅓ cup (80 mL) microgreens, for garnish

This dish is a true gem. Thinly sliced vibrant beets lay the foundation for this exquisite carpaccio. The pesto, with its unique twist, combines the earthy sweetness of roasted carrots with the nutty richness of pine nuts, resulting in a burst of flavors that complements the beets perfectly. The addition of carrots to the pesto adds a playful touch, infusing it with a vibrant orange hue and a hint of sweetness that elevates any dish. Make sure to make extra to add to other recipes.

Preheat the oven to 400°F (200°C).

Using a sharp knife or preferably a mandoline, slice the beets very thin and arrange on a serving platter.

Make the pesto: Place the carrots on a sheet pan, season with salt and pepper, and drizzle with 2 tablespoons (30 mL) olive oil. Roast for about 20 minutes, or until the carrots begin to soften and brown. Remove from the oven and set aside to cool slightly.

Add the basil, garlic, ¾ cup (180 mL) olive oil, lemon juice, and ½ teaspoon (2.5 mL) salt to a high-speed blender and pulse to chop roughly. Add the carrots and pulse to combine. Add the pine nuts, walnuts, nutritional yeast, and 1 teaspoon (5 mL) pepper and pulse to a chunky paste. Adjust salt and pepper to taste.

Spoon the pesto over the beet carpaccio, drizzle with olive oil, and garnish with the microgreens.

RUSTIC HERB AND SEED CRACKERS

MAKES 40 CRACKERS • COOK TIME: 30 MINUTES
PREP TIME: 20 MINUTES, PLUS 2 HOURS RESTING TIME

½ cup (125 mL) rolled oats

½ cup (125 mL) sunflower seeds

½ cup (125 mL) pumpkin seeds

¼ cup (60 mL) flaxseeds

¼ cup (60 mL) sesame seeds

½ cup (125 mL) raw buckwheat

¼ cup (60 mL) chia seeds

½ cup (125 mL) hemp seeds

2 tablespoons (30 mL) psyllium

1 teaspoon (5 mL) chopped fresh rosemary leaves

½ teaspoon (2.5 mL) chopped fresh thyme leaves

freshly ground black pepper

1 teaspoon (5 mL) kosher salt

2 tablespoons (30 mL) extra-virgin olive oil

flaky sea salt

Once you discover how effortless it is to make your own crackers, you'll never settle for store-bought ones again. These homemade crackers are a testament to simplicity and taste, making them an irresistible snack or an accompaniment to your favorite dips and spreads.

In a large bowl, combine the oats, sunflower seeds, pumpkin seeds, flaxseeds, sesame seeds, buckwheat, chia seeds, hemp seeds, psyllium, rosemary, thyme, a few grinds of pepper, and the salt. Add 1½ cups (375 mL) warm water and the olive oil and stir well. Cover and allow it to rest in the fridge for at least 2 hours.

When you are ready to bake the crackers, preheat the oven to 350°F (180°C) and place a rack in the middle and top position.

Divide the dough into two equal parts and put one-half on a sheet of parchment paper large enough to fit on a medium sheet pan. Place another piece of parchment paper the same size on top to sandwich the dough between the parchment. Gently squash the dough down and, using a rolling pin, spread it flat all the way to the edges. The dough should cover the parchment paper exactly. Repeat with the other half of the dough.

Slide the cracker dough onto two sheet pans and peel off the top layer of parchment. Sprinkle with flaky sea salt. Bake for 20 minutes, turning the pans after 10 minutes to ensure even cooking.

Remove from the oven and flip the crackers over. Remove the parchment paper. Return to the oven for another 10 minutes to crisp. Remove from the oven, allow to cool slightly, and break into pieces.

Serve with dips and a vegan cheese board.

HIBISCUS-BLOOD ORANGE SPRITZ

SERVES 10 TO 12 • PREP TIME: 10 MINUTES, PLUS 1 HOUR TO STEEP

⅓ cup (80 mL) dried hibiscus flowers

6 tablespoons (90 mL) granulated sugar

2 cups (500 mL) freshly squeezed or store-bought
    blood orange juice

1 bottle (750 mL) Prosecco or mineral water

Whether you're looking to unwind after a long day or impress your guests at a backyard gathering, the Hibiscus–Blood Orange Spritz is the ideal choice. The vivid crimson hue of the drink, derived from steeping dried hibiscus flowers, adds a touch of elegance and sophistication to any occasion. For those who prefer a nonalcoholic version, replace the Prosecco with mineral water and allow the natural flavors to shine. The combination of hibiscus and blood orange is enough to create a refreshing mocktail that will keep you cool on even the hottest summer nights.

In a small saucepan, bring 1 cup (250 mL) water to a boil over high heat. When boiling, remove from the heat and add the hibiscus flowers and sugar. Stir well to dissolve the sugar and let steep, covered, for about 1 hour. Strain the hibiscus concentrate and store it in a bottle or jar in the fridge. Discard the used hibiscus flowers.

In individual glasses, combine 1 part hibiscus concentrate, 1 part blood orange juice, and 2 parts Prosecco over ice.

CRUMBED ARTICHOKES
WITH CASHEW AIOLI

SERVES 4 TO 6 • COOK TIME: 15 MINUTES
PREP TIME: 20 MINUTES, PLUS 30 MINUTES TO 1 HOUR TO SOAK THE CASHEWS

FOR THE AIOLI

½ cup (125 mL) raw cashews soaked in hot water
for 30 minutes to 1 hour or overnight

½ cup (125 mL) unsweetened almond milk

2 fresh garlic cloves or 2 roasted garlic cloves
for a more mellow flavor

2 tablespoons (30 mL) freshly squeezed lemon juice

½ teaspoon (2.5 mL) smoked paprika,
plus more for garnish

2 tablespoons (30 mL) nutritional yeast

1 tablespoon (15 mL) extra-virgin olive oil

½ teaspoon (2.5 mL) kosher salt

chopped fresh chives, for garnish

FOR THE CRUMBED ARTICHOKES

½ cup (125 mL) cornstarch

½ cup (125 mL) aquafaba (canned chickpea liquid)

1½ cups (375 mL) panko bread crumbs

¼ cup (60 mL) nutritional yeast

1 teaspoon (5 mL) smoked paprika

½ teaspoon (2.5 mL) onion powder

½ teaspoon (2.5 mL) garlic powder

1 teaspoon (5 mL) kosher salt

freshly ground black pepper

one 12-ounce (340 g) jar marinated artichoke hearts,
drained and halved

5 tablespoons (75 mL) grapeseed oil
or other neutral-flavored oil, for frying

flaky sea salt

lemon wedges

This recipe is designed to impress your guests without causing any stress in the kitchen. With just a few simple steps, you can create a crowd-pleasing appetizer that will have everyone reaching for more. The artichoke hearts are coated in a flavorful crumb mixture, then fried to golden perfection, resulting in a satisfyingly crunchy exterior. But what truly takes this dish to the next level is the creamy cashew aioli. Made with just a handful of ingredients, it's a rich and tangy sauce that perfectly complements the artichokes.

Make the aioli: To a high-speed blender, add the cashews, almond milk, garlic, lemon juice, paprika, nutritional yeast, olive oil, and salt and blend until super smooth and creamy. Transfer to a serving bowl and garnish with chopped chives and a sprinkle of paprika.

Make the artichokes: Set up the breading station by placing the cornstarch on a plate and the aquafaba in a shallow bowl. Whisk together the panko, nutritional yeast, paprika, onion powder, garlic powder, kosher salt, and a few grinds of pepper on another large plate.

Dip the artichoke hearts first into the cornstarch to coat well, next into the aquafaba, and finally into the panko mixture.

Heat the oil in a cast-iron skillet or heavy-bottomed pan over medium heat. When it starts to shimmer, add the artichoke hearts and cook for about 8 minutes, or until golden brown and crispy on all sides.

Serve hot, sprinkled with flaky sea salt and topped with the aioli, with lemon wedges on the side.

BUCKWHEAT BLINIS WITH CARROT "SMOKED SALMON" AND CREAM CHEESE

MAKES 12 TO 15; SERVES 4 • PREP TIME: 30 MINUTES • COOK TIME: 30 MINUTES

FOR THE CARROT "SMOKED SALMON"

¼ teaspoon (1.25 mL) mustard seeds

¼ teaspoon (1.25 mL) mixed peppercorns

¼ teaspoon (1.25 mL) coriander seeds

1 piece kombu seaweed (optional)

2 tablespoons (30 mL) granulated sugar

¼ cup (60 mL) apple cider vinegar

¼ cup (60 mL) white wine vinegar

1 large carrot

½ medium red onion, thinly sliced

FOR THE BLINIS

½ cup (125 mL) spelt flour

¼ cup (60 mL) buckwheat flour

¼ teaspoon (1.25 mL) baking soda

½ teaspoon (2.5 mL) baking powder

kosher salt

½ cup (125 mL) unsweetened oat milk

1 tablespoon (15 mL) maple syrup

extra-virgin olive oil

FOR SERVING

¼ cup (60 mL) vegan cream cheese

¼ cup (60 mL) drained capers (optional)

thinly sliced pickled red onions
(see Note, page 181)

a few fresh dill sprigs

CHLOÉ WRITES: We absolutely love apéro, and this recipe is the perfect addition to this special moment of the day. It adds a delicious touch to any occasion, especially when paired with a bottle of Champagne. When I'm in charge of the apéro at a party, I often bring these along. It's a fun and interactive dish where everyone can make their own. Personally, I like extra cream cheese and dill to add a burst of flavor.

Make the carrot "smoked salmon": Place the mustard seeds, peppercorns, coriander seeds, kombu, if using, sugar, apple cider vinegar, white wine vinegar, and 1½ cups (375 mL) water in a medium saucepan and bring to a boil over high heat. Once boiling, reduce the heat to medium-low.

Using a mandoline or vegetable peeler, carefully slice the carrot lengthwise, add to the pot along with the onion, and simmer until the carrot is lightly cooked and pliable but still a vibrant color, about 10 minutes. Remove from the heat, allow to cool, and store in the refrigerator until ready to use. When ready to use, drain the carrot and discard the onion.

Make the blinis: In a medium bowl, whisk together the spelt flour, buckwheat flour, baking soda, baking powder, and a pinch of salt. Make a well in the middle, add the oat milk and maple syrup, and gently fold together to combine. Let rest for 10 minutes. ➳

↞ Heat a large frying pan over high heat. When hot (sprinkle a drop of water into the pan; it should sizzle and disappear immediately), drizzle with olive oil and, using a tablespoon, scoop dollops of the blini mixture into the pan. Cook in batches until the blinis bubble and set, 1 to 2 minutes. Flip and cook on the other side for 30 seconds.

Serve the cooled blinis topped with 1 teaspoon each of cream cheese, carrot "smoked salmon," capers, if using, pickled onions, and dill.

FOCACCIA WITH FRESH FIGS AND OLIVES

SERVES 6 TO 8 • PREP TIME: 35 MINUTES • COOK TIME: 20 TO 25 MINUTES

5 tablespoons (75 mL) extra-virgin olive oil, divided

3 cups (750 mL) all-purpose flour

1½ teaspoons (7.5 mL) kosher salt

one ¼-ounce (7 g) packet instant yeast

6 fresh figs, sliced lengthwise into 18 pieces

½ cup (125 mL) kalamata olives, pitted and sliced

1 cup (250 mL) thinly sliced red onion

flaky sea salt

fresh thyme, for garnish (optional)

This focaccia is perfect for the apéro, easy to make and so delicious with the addition of fresh figs to the recipe. No fresh figs at the market? Not a problem, as it works well with many other toppings, such as fresh tomatoes or red peppers and a dusting of vegan parmesan.

Preheat the oven to 450°F (230°C) and grease a 9-by-13-inch baking sheet with high sides with 3 tablespoons (45 mL) olive oil.

In a large mixing bowl, whisk together the flour, kosher salt, and yeast.

Make a well in the center of the dry ingredients and pour in 1½ cups (375 mL) water and 1 tablespoon (15 mL) olive oil. Mix until a sticky dough forms.

Transfer the dough to the prepared baking sheet and spread it out evenly using your hands. Cover with plastic wrap and let the dough rise for 20 minutes.

Once the dough has doubled in size, remove the plastic wrap and, using your fingers, press into the dough, helping it expand even more. Use your fingers to create dimples all over the dough.

Press the figs, olives, and onion into the dough, distributing them evenly.

Drizzle the remaining 1 tablespoon (15 mL) olive oil over the focaccia, sprinkle with flaky sea salt, and bake for 20 to 25 minutes, until golden brown. Remove the focaccia from the oven and let cool slightly in the pan before transferring to a wire rack to cool completely.

Top with fresh thyme, if using. Slice the focaccia and serve warm or at room temperature.

TRUDY WRITES: Whenever Chloé visits Montreal, we prioritize carving out time for a special date. It's a cherished moment when we can be alone and free from distractions and catch up on each other's lives. Despite our daily FaceTime conversations, this date allows us to exchange on a more intimate level, diving deeper into meaningful conversations and creating lasting memories.

Date night isn't limited to romantic partners; it extends to best friends, family members, and anyone else with whom you feel close to. It could be an opportunity to forge a new friendship or rekindle a relationship with an old acquaintance. Regardless of who accompanies you, the potential for an interesting and meaningful experience is ever present.

One of the best things about date night is preparing the meal together: collaborating in the kitchen, creating new recipes, sharing tasks, and exchanging laughter as you bring each dish to life. There's a sense of togetherness and shared accomplishment that comes from this joint effort.

In the end, date nights provide an opportunity to nourish not only our bodies with a good meal but also our souls with genuine connection. They remind us of the importance of carving out a moment with the special people in our lives, creating memories that will withstand the test of time.

CAULIFLOWER PARMESAN STEAKS WITH CHIMICHURRI

SERVES 2 · PREP TIME: 20 MINUTES · COOK TIME: 30 MINUTES

1 large cauliflower head,
  cut vertically into large steaklike slices

¾ cup (180 mL) extra-virgin olive oil

FOR THE CHIMICHURRI

2 cups (500 mL) firmly packed fresh Italian
  parsley leaves

½ cup (125 mL) fresh oregano leaves

4 garlic cloves

¼ cup (60 mL) red wine vinegar

2 tablespoons (30 mL) freshly squeezed lemon juice

1 teaspoon (5 mL) finely chopped red chili pepper

1 teaspoon (5 mL) kosher salt

1 teaspoon (5 mL) freshly ground black pepper

FOR SERVING

2 tablespoons (30 mL) vegan parmesan cheese

2 scallions, thinly sliced on the diagonal

½ cup (125 mL) thinly sliced fresh radishes

Our spicy chimichurri is a flavor explosion that adds a kick to every bite. Packed with fresh ingredients, this vibrant sauce takes the cauliflower parmesan steak to a whole new level. The heat from the hot pepper balances the dish beautifully, leaving you craving more of its addictive flavor. This is such an easy, satisfying dish to make as you add more plant-based meals into your routine.

Preheat the oven to 400°F (200°C) (see Note).

Coat both sides of the cauliflower with the oil and place on a rimmed baking sheet. Bake for about 25 minutes, or until the cauliflower is nicely crisp and can easily be cut through with a knife.

Meanwhile, make the chimichurri: To a blender or food processor, add the parsley, oregano, garlic, vinegar, lemon juice, chili pepper, salt, and pepper. Pulse 4 times at 3-second intervals or until the desired consistency is reached.

Place the roasted cauliflower steaks on a serving platter. Brush each steak liberally with the chimichurri, and sprinkle with the parmesan. Top with the scallions and radishes.

NOTE: *You can also use an air fryer to roast the cauliflower steaks. Set the air fryer at 385°F (195°C) and roast for 16 minutes.*

STORAGE: *This recipe makes 2 cups of chimichurri, perfect for leftovers, which can be used in other recipes, see Grilled Baguette with Caramelized Mushrooms, Balsamic Tahini Butter, and Shaved Parmesan (page 205) and Sweet Potato and Endive Salad (page 225). Store in an airtight container in the fridge for up to a week.*

TOFU SCHNITZEL WITH COLESLAW

SERVES 2 TO 4 · PREP TIME: 25 MINUTES · COOK TIME: 15 MINUTES

16 ounces (454 g) extra-firm tofu

one 15.5-ounce (439 g) can chickpeas

1½ cups (375 mL) shaved cabbage

1 medium carrot, grated

½ medium green apple, thinly sliced

1 scallion, thinly sliced

handful of fresh Italian parsley leaves

1 cup (250 mL) panko bread crumbs

¼ cup (60 mL) nutritional yeast

½ teaspoon (2.5 mL) onion powder

½ teaspoon (2.5 mL) garlic powder

1 teaspoon (5 mL) chopped fresh rosemary leaves

1 teaspoon (5 mL) fresh thyme leaves

1 teaspoon (5 mL) kosher salt

freshly ground black pepper

¼ cup (60 mL) cornstarch

¼ cup (60 mL) grapeseed oil
  or other neutral-flavored oil

1 tablespoon (15 mL) drained capers,
  for garnish (optional)

4 small radishes, sliced (optional)

FOR THE LEMON-CAPER DRESSING

¼ cup (60 mL) freshly squeezed lemon juice

6 tablespoons (90 mL) extra-virgin olive oil

3 tablespoons (45 mL) chopped fresh Italian parsley

1 garlic clove

1 teaspoon (5 mL) maple syrup

1 teaspoon (5 mL) Dijon mustard

CHLOÉ WRITES: When my mother first adopted a plant-based diet, she was skeptical about incorporating tofu into her meals. She considered it to be bland and lacking in flavor and had difficulty turning it into a delicious dish. However, I introduced her to the secret of elevating tofu using the perfect technique and spices. Now tofu is one of her favorite ingredients to work with. This recipe holds a special place among our all-time favorites. Complemented by a refreshing coleslaw that adds a delightful crunch, this dish is the perfect summer meal.

Wrap the tofu in a kitchen towel, place it between two sheet pans, and put a heavy weight, such as a cast-iron skillet or canned beans, on top. Press for at least 15 minutes to extract any liquid.

Into a shallow bowl, strain and reserve the liquid (aquafaba) from the chickpeas. (Save the chickpeas for Spicy Crispy Chickpeas on page 33.)

Make the coleslaw: In a medium bowl, toss together the cabbage, carrot, apple, scallion, and parsley. Set aside.

On a large plate, combine the panko, nutritional yeast, onion powder, garlic powder, rosemary, thyme, salt, and a few grinds of pepper and mix well. Place the cornstarch on a separate plate.

Cut the tofu block into 4 slices lengthwise. Coat one tofu slice with the cornstarch, dip it into the aquafaba, and then press firmly into the panko mixture, coating both sides and the edges to get a nice thick coating. Press down again to make sure the coating adheres to the slice. Repeat with the remaining slices. ➻

↤ Line a plate with paper towels. In a cast-iron skillet or heavy-bottomed pan, heat the grapeseed oil over medium heat. When it starts to shimmer, fry the tofu in batches until golden brown, 3 to 4 minutes each side. Remove from the pan and drain on the prepared plate.

Make the dressing: To a high-speed blender, add the lemon juice, olive oil, parsley, garlic, maple syrup, and mustard and blend until smooth.

Toss the coleslaw with half the dressing and drizzle the remaining dressing over the tofu schnitzel. Garnish with the capers and radishes if desired.

WHITE BEAN AND CAULIFLOWER PURÉE WITH ROASTED VEGETABLES AND BALSAMIC DRESSING

SERVES 2 • PREP TIME: 15 MINUTES • COOK TIME: 40 MINUTES

1 medium eggplant, cut into 1½-inch slices

1 medium red bell pepper, cut into 1½-inch pieces

1 medium green bell pepper, cut into 1½-inch pieces

1 medium yellow bell pepper, cut into 1½-inch pieces

½ medium red onion, cut into ½-inch pieces

1 medium zucchini, sliced

¼ cup (60 mL) extra-virgin olive oil

kosher salt and freshly ground black pepper

FOR THE WHITE BEAN AND CAULIFLOWER PURÉE

2 tablespoons (30 mL) extra-virgin olive oil

1 small onion, diced

2 garlic cloves, chopped

2 bay leaves

1 fresh rosemary sprig

1 cup (250 mL) chopped cauliflower florets

one 15.5-ounce (439 g) can cannellini beans, drained and rinsed

½ teaspoon (2.5 mL) kosher salt

freshly ground black pepper

½ cup (125 mL) plant milk, such as almond or soy

1 teaspoon (5 mL) nutritional yeast

fresh basil leaves, for garnish

FOR THE BALSAMIC DRESSING

2 tablespoons (30 mL) balsamic vinegar

3 tablespoons (45 mL) extra-virgin olive oil

1 teaspoon (5 mL) maple syrup

1 teaspoon (5 mL) Dijon mustard

1 small garlic clove, finely grated

kosher salt and freshly ground black pepper

TRUDY WRITES: Imagine a cozy evening at home where you and your date want to cook something simple, yet elegant. I promise you, this recipe is just that and will make your night unforgettable. It holds a special place in my heart, as it has become our go-to meal whenever we want to be a little fancy, without any fuss. The harmony of flavors perfectly complements the warmth and intimacy of an evening well spent with a special person.

Preheat the oven to 400°F (200°C).

In a medium bowl, toss together the eggplant, the red, green, and yellow bell peppers, the onion, and zucchini with the olive oil. Season with salt and pepper, and place on a large sheet pan. Roast for 35 to 40 minutes, until the eggplant has softened and starts to color slightly. Remove from the oven and set aside.

Make the purée: In a medium pot with a lid, heat the olive oil over medium heat. When it starts to shimmer, add the onion, garlic, bay leaves, and rosemary and cook, stirring, until the onion has softened and becomes translucent, about 5 minutes. Add the cauliflower and cook, stirring, for 3 to 4 minutes. Add the beans and season with the salt and a few grinds of pepper. Stir in the plant milk and ½ cup (125 mL) water, cover, and cook for 5 minutes.

Remove the lid and continue to cook an additional 8 to 10 minutes, until the cauliflower has softened. Sprinkle in the nutritional yeast, stir, and remove from the heat. Discard the bay leaves and rosemary sprig and, using an immersion blender, blend until smooth and creamy (see Note). ➤

COMESTIBLES

Comestibles Can Bernat

Panets
BOCADILLOS
Sandwiches

Refrescs
REFRESCOS
Soft Drinks

Tabac
TABACO
Tobacco

Cafè per endur
CAFÉ PARA LLEVAR
Coffee to go

Gelats
HELADOS
ice cream

↢ *Make the dressing:* Place the vinegar, olive oil, maple syrup, mustard, and garlic into a jar. Season with salt and pepper to taste and shake vigorously until emulsified. Toss the roasted veggies with the balsamic dressing and serve on top of the purée. Garnish with basil leaves.

NOTE: *If you do not have an immersion blender, transfer to a standing blender in batches and blend until smooth and creamy.*

TIRAMISÙ FOR TWO

SERVES 2 TO 4 • PREP TIME: 20 MINUTES, PLUS 2 HOURS OR OVERNIGHT TO SET

1 cup (250 mL) extra-strong coffee

1 tablespoon (15 mL) coconut sugar

8 ounces (227 g) silken tofu

½ cup (125 mL) unsweetened coconut cream

½ cup (125 mL) raw cashews,
    soaked overnight (see Note)

¼ cup (60 mL) maple syrup

1 teaspoon (5 mL) vanilla extract

flaky sea salt

one 7.5-ounce (200 g) packet plain vegan cookies,
    such as graham crackers or digestives

2 tablespoons (30 mL) cacao powder

CHLOÉ WRITES: I'm a huge fan of desserts, and let me tell you, tiramisù is hands down my favorite. My mom had never even tried making it before, and honestly, she wasn't sure if she'd even like it. But when we were brainstorming recipes for our book, I managed to convince her that tiramisù had to be included. And now it's become one of her go-to treats to serve when hosting. To make it even more special, we like to serve it in old wineglasses or vintage bowls, adding a little extra flair.

Prepare the extra-strong coffee and dissolve the coconut sugar in it while still warm. Put the coffee into the fridge to cool.

Wrap the tofu in a few paper towel sheets. Press between two plates for at least 15 minutes to soak up some of the excess liquid.

To a high-speed blender, add the tofu, coconut cream, cashews, maple syrup, vanilla, and a pinch of sea salt and blend until super smooth and creamy.

When ready to assemble, pour the coffee into a shallow dish or bowl. Begin the bottom layer of the tiramisù by soaking the cookies in the coffee one by one, turning them in the coffee for about 10 seconds so they are soaked with coffee but not falling apart. Layer the cookies on the bottom of two wide glasses or jars, then dollop some of the cashew cream on top. Repeat with the remaining cookies and cream for about 3 or 4 layers of each, or until you reach the top of the glasses or jars. Dust the top with cacao powder and refrigerate for at least 2 hours or up to overnight before serving.

NOTE: *You can fast-track the cashews by soaking them in boiling-hot water for 30 minutes to an hour.*

PAPPARDELLE MUSHROOM BOLOGNESE

SERVES 4 • PREP TIME: 15 MINUTES • COOK TIME: 1 HOUR 10 MINUTES

1½ cups (375 mL) cremini mushrooms, stems removed

1½ cups (375 mL) Swiss brown mushrooms, stems removed

4 tablespoons (60 mL) extra-virgin olive oil, divided, plus more for the pasta

kosher salt and freshly ground black pepper

1 medium yellow onion, finely chopped

2 garlic cloves, finely chopped

½ large carrot, finely chopped

½ celery stalk, finely chopped

2 tablespoons (30 mL) tomato paste

4 sun-dried tomatoes, finely chopped

2 bay leaves

1 fresh rosemary sprig

one 14.5-ounce (411 g) can crushed tomatoes

3 or 4 fresh vegan lasagna sheets, cut into 1½-inch strips

2 tablespoons (30 mL) vegan parmesan, for garnish

3 tablespoons (45 mL) fresh Italian parsley leaves, finely chopped, for garnish

CHLOÉ SAYS: This easy, delicious recipe is perfect for a date night. The joy of cooking with your partner or friend while chatting and preparing the meal makes it even more special. When Trudy and her partner first met, he would always cook a version of this meal. It's a foolproof dish that adds an extra touch of magic to time well spent.

Preheat the oven to 400°F (200°C) and line a sheet pan with parchment paper.

Place the cremini and Swiss mushrooms on the prepared sheet pan, drizzle with 2 tablespoons (30 mL) olive oil, and season with salt and pepper. Roast in the oven for 25 minutes. Remove the roasted mushrooms from the oven and allow to cool slightly.

While the mushrooms are roasting, heat the remaining 2 tablespoons (30 mL) olive oil in a large saucepan. When it starts to shimmer, add the onion and garlic and cook, stirring, until the onion becomes translucent, about 3 minutes. Add the carrot, celery, tomato paste, sun-dried tomatoes, bay leaves, and rosemary and cook, stirring frequently, for 10 minutes.

Finely chop the roasted mushrooms, add to the pan along with the crushed tomatoes, and season to taste with salt and pepper. Stir well, reduce the heat to medium-low, and simmer until all the liquid has been absorbed, about 45 minutes. Remove the bay leaves and rosemary sprig before serving.

Meanwhile, bring a medium pot of water to a boil. Cook the pasta per the package directions until al dente. Drain and sprinkle with a little olive oil. Serve with the mushroom Bolognese, parmesan, and a sprinkle of parsley.

CHARRED ASPARAGUS AND BROCCOLINI ON ROMESCO SAUCE

SERVES 2 TO 4 · PREP TIME: 5 MINUTES · COOK TIME: 20 MINUTES

1 bunch asparagus, woody ends removed

1 bunch broccolini

1 tablespoon (15 mL) extra-virgin olive oil, plus 2 teaspoons (10 mL) for drizzle

1 teaspoon (5 mL) kosher salt

1 teaspoon (5 mL) freshly ground black pepper

1 cup (250 mL) store-bought vegan Romesco sauce

1 cup (250 mL) microgreens, for garnish

⅓ cup (80 mL) roasted pistachios, crushed, for garnish

Perfect as an appetizer or side, this charred asparagus and broccolini recipe has a satisfying crunch. The velvety Romesco sauce enhances the dish with its roasted red pepper and nutty undertones. Whether you're looking to elevate a cozy dinner or planning a romantic date for two, this recipe is guaranteed to set the stage for an unforgettable evening.

Preheat the oven to 375°F (190°C) or heat the grill.

On a large sheet pan, toss the asparagus and broccolini with 1 tablespoon (15 mL) olive oil and the salt and pepper. Roast for 15 to 20 minutes, until the vegetables are cooked and the edges are crispy. (If preparing on the grill, cook for 3 to 4 minutes on each side over a medium flame.)

Smear the Romesco sauce on a large platter and arrange the asparagus and broccolini on top. Drizzle with 2 teaspoons (10 mL) olive oil and garnish with the microgreens and pistachios.

POLENTA WITH WHITE BEANS AND TOMATOES

SERVES 2 TO 4 · PREP TIME: 15 MINUTES · COOK TIME: 35 MINUTES

1 cup (250 mL) polenta

1 teaspoon (5 mL) kosher salt,
    divided, plus more to taste

½ cup (125 mL) vegan parmesan

2 tablespoons (30 mL) vegan butter, melted

one 15.5-ounce (439 g) can cannellini beans,
    drained and rinsed

1 cup (250 mL) diced red onion

2 cups (500 mL) cherry tomatoes, halved

2 garlic cloves, crushed

2 tablespoons (30 mL) extra-virgin olive oil

2 tablespoons (30 mL) freshly squeezed lemon juice

2 fresh rosemary sprigs, stems removed,
    plus 1 teaspoon finely chopped leaves for garnish

1 teaspoon (5 mL) freshly ground black pepper,
    plus more to taste

½ teaspoon (2.5 mL) herbes de Provence

fresh baguette (optional)

As we prepared this meal for the book, we were in a cozy cottage perched on the hillside town of Biniaraix in Mallorca. The sun wrapped us in its comforting warmth as we sat down to eat, and we couldn't help but admire the stunning view of the valley below while savoring each flavor of this dish. In that moment, we knew it was a memory that would forever hold a special place in our hearts.

In a large pot, bring 4 cups (1 L) water to a boil over high heat, add the polenta, and reduce the heat to a simmer. Whisk the polenta every couple of minutes to avoid lumps until it starts to thicken. Cover and cook, whisking every 5 minutes, until the grains are tender and the polenta is creamy, about 30 minutes. Remove from the heat and add ½ teaspoon (2.25 mL) salt, the parmesan, and butter, whisking continually. Once they are completely incorporated, cover and set aside.

While the polenta is cooking, to a medium skillet add the cannellini beans, onion, tomatoes, garlic, olive oil, lemon juice, rosemary sprigs, ½ teaspoon (2.25 mL) salt, pepper, and herbes de Provence and stir to combine. Cook, stirring halfway through, for 25 minutes. Once cooked, serve over the polenta with a sprinkle of the chopped rosemary, salt and pepper to taste, and the fresh baguette, if using.

CILANTRO RICE VEGGIE BOWL

SERVES 2 TO 4 • PREP TIME: 15 MINUTES • COOK TIME: 30 MINUTES

1 cup (250 mL) white basmati rice

⅓ cup (80 mL) firmly packed chopped
    fresh cilantro leaves

kosher salt and freshly ground black pepper

1 medium butternut squash, peeled, cubed,
    and seeds reserved

4½ tablespoons (67.5 mL) extra-virgin olive oil, divided

10 asparagus spears, woody ends removed

½ cup (125 mL) roughly chopped white onion

1 cup (250 mL) green cabbage, chopped lengthwise

1½ cups (375 mL) cherry tomatoes, halved

4 to 6 medium marinated artichoke hearts,
    halved or quartered, for topping

⅓ cup (80 mL) crumbled vegan feta, for topping

½ cup (125 mL) assorted olives, such as kalamata
    and green, for topping

FOR THE BALSAMIC TAHINI DRESSING

⅓ cup (80 mL) tahini

3 tablespoons (45 mL) extra-virgin olive oil

2 tablespoons (30 mL) balsamic glaze or reduction

1 tablespoon (15 mL) nutritional yeast

1 tablespoon (15 mL) Dijon mustard

CHLOÉ WRITES: This is the ultimate date night staple, born of creativity and a desire to use up all the lingering ingredients in my fridge. It's the perfect solution for an easy dinner when you need a nourishing dish that can be whipped up in no time. If you don't have all the exact ingredients, don't be afraid to improvise and replace certain vegetables. Get creative.

Preheat the oven to 400°F (200°C).

Rinse the rice thoroughly until the water runs clear. Place in a medium pot with a lid with 2 cups (500 mL) water, cover, and bring to a boil over high heat. When boiling, turn the heat down to low and simmer for 10 to 12 minutes, until the rice is cooked, according to the package directions.

Turn the heat off, add the cilantro, season with salt and pepper to taste, and stir well. Let sit, covered, for 5 minutes.

On a large baking sheet, sprinkle the butternut squash with 1 table-spoon (15 mL) olive oil, season with salt and pepper, and bake for 10 minutes. Meanwhile, coat the asparagus with 1 tablespoon (15 mL) olive oil, season with salt and pepper, and set aside. Mix the reserved seeds with ½ tablespoon (7.5 mL) olive oil, season with salt and pepper, and set aside. Remove the squash from the oven and add the asparagus and seeds to the same pan, separated, and bake for an additional 15 minutes; the squash and asparagus should be cooked and the seeds lightly browned and crispy. Remove from the oven and set aside. ➜

← Heat the remaining 2 tablespoons (30 mL) olive oil in a small pan over medium heat. When it starts to shimmer, add the onion and cook, stirring, until it starts to turn golden, 3 to 4 minutes. Add the cabbage and tomatoes to the pan and cook, stirring, until the cabbage has softened and the tomatoes are cooked through, 4 to 5 minutes. Season with salt and pepper to taste.

Make the dressing: In a small bowl whisk together the tahini, olive oil, balsamic glaze, nutritional yeast, and mustard. Stir in 2 to 4 tablespoons (30 to 60 mL) water as needed to achieve a smooth consistency.

Layer each serving bowl with the rice, roasted squash and asparagus, and the sautéed cabbage, onion, and tomatoes. Top with the marinated artichoke hearts, vegan feta, olives, and roasted squash seeds.

Finalize the dish with a drizzle of the dressing.

FRESH TOMATO THIN-CRUST PIZZA

SERVES 2 • PREP TIME: 20 MINUTES • COOK TIME: 15 TO 20 MINUTES

2 tablespoons (130 mL) extra-virgin olive oil, divided, plus more for the pan

5 pearl onions

pizza or flatbread dough, at room temperature

1 cup (250 mL) olive tapenade

1 cup (250 mL) sun-dried tomatoes in oil, sliced lengthwise

3 medium heirloom tomatoes

½ cup (125 mL) cherry tomatoes, halved

fresh basil leaves, for garnish

½ cup (125 mL) edible flowers, for garnish (optional)

Pizza is truly the best meal ever. It's the one dish that brings people together, ignites joy, and leaves you craving another slice. This recipe celebrates the vibrant flavors of fresh tomatoes, allowing them to take center stage. The burst of tangy, juicy tomatoes will make you realize that sometimes simplicity is the key.

Preheat the oven to 400°F (200°C). Oil a pizza pan and set aside.

On a small sheet pan, drizzle the pearl onions with 1 tablespoon (15 mL) olive oil and roast for 10 to 15 minutes, until translucent.

Meanwhile, stretch the pizza dough into the shape of the pizza pan and place onto the prepared pan. Spread the tapenade evenly over the dough, then top with the sun-dried tomatoes. Slice the heirloom tomatoes and top the pizza with them. Bake for 15 to 20 minutes, until the crust is golden brown. While the pizza is baking, halve the roasted pearl onions.

Remove the pizza from the oven and top with the cherry tomatoes, roasted pearl onions, basil, and edible flowers, if using, and drizzle with the remaining 1 tablespoon (15 mL) olive oil.

ROASTED TOMATO AND RED PEPPER SOUP

SERVES 4 TO 6 • PREP TIME: 15 MINUTES • COOK TIME: 50 MINUTES

2 large red bell peppers, halved and seeded

3 large tomatoes, halved

2 tablespoons (30 mL) extra-virgin olive oil, plus more as needed

1 large red onion, quartered

2 garlic cloves, minced

1 teaspoon (5 mL) ground cumin

1 teaspoon (5 mL) smoked paprika

1 teaspoon (5 mL) turmeric

1 teaspoon (5 mL) kosher salt

1 teaspoon (5 mL) freshly ground black pepper

3 cups (750 mL) vegetable broth

1 cup (250 mL) oat milk

FOR THE TAHINI SWIRL

2 tablespoons (30 mL) tahini

1 tablespoon (15 mL) extra-virgin olive oil

2 teaspoons (10 mL) balsamic vinegar

1 teaspoon (5 mL) ground cumin

1 teaspoon (5 mL) ground sumac

Is there a better duo than tomato soup and a grilled cheese sandwich? We didn't think so. We are all about a comfort meal, and this is the one we always go back to. What sets this soup apart from traditional tomato soup is the delightful twist brought by the addition of red bell peppers. Though tomatoes provide a classic base, peppers introduce a new dimension of flavor and depth, infusing the soup with a subtle smokiness and a touch of sweetness and balancing the tanginess of the tomatoes perfectly. This combination creates a soup that is both familiar and exciting, making it a delicious hearty dish.

Preheat the oven to 400°F (200°C).

Place the bell peppers and tomatoes on a large baking sheet, drizzle with olive oil, and roast for 20 to 25 minutes, until the peppers are soft and charred on both sides.

Heat 2 tablespoons (30 mL) olive oil in a large pot over high heat. When it starts to shimmer, add the onion and garlic and cook, stirring, until softened, about 5 minutes. Add the cumin, paprika, turmeric, salt, and pepper and stir to combine. Add the roasted peppers and tomatoes and stir to coat with the spices.

Add the vegetable broth and oat milk and bring to a boil. Reduce the heat to medium-low and let simmer for 25 minutes.

Make the tahini swirl: In a small bowl, combine the tahini, olive oil, balsamic vinegar, cumin, and sumac and mix well.

Remove the pot from the heat and blend the soup until smooth using an immersion blender or in batches using a standing blender. Serve in individual bowls, topped with tahini swirl.

HERBY FARRO WITH ROASTED VEGGIES

SERVES 2 TO 4 · PREP TIME: 10 MINUTES · COOK TIME: 30 MINUTES

1 cup (250 mL) pearled farro

3½ tablespoons (52.5 mL) extra-virgin olive oil, divided

¼ cup (60 mL) roughly chopped fresh Italian parsley leaves

2 cups (500 mL) diced butternut squash

1 cup (250 mL) diced yellow zucchini

6 medium Brussels sprouts, ends trimmed, outer leaves removed, and halved

1 teaspoon (5 mL) dried thyme

1 teaspoon (5 mL) herbes de Provence

kosher salt and freshly ground black pepper

4 cups (1 L) firmly packed arugula

1 tablespoon (15 mL) pumpkin seeds, for garnish

1 tablespoon (15 mL) sunflower seeds, for garnish

FOR THE DRESSING

1 cup (250 mL) firmly packed fresh basil leaves

3 tablespoons (45 mL) extra-virgin olive oil

2 tablespoons (30 mL) nutritional yeast

1 tablespoon (15 mL) Dijon mustard

1 tablespoon (15 mL) freshly squeezed lemon juice

1 tablespoon (15 mL) vegan parmesan

1½ tablespoons (22.5 mL) balsamic vinegar

Imagine a cold winter evening. Snow is gently falling outside, and you're seated at a table with a loved one. This is what we pictured when creating this recipe: something hearty and soothing. The nutty farro, infused with parsley, is perfectly complemented by the caramelized sweetness of the roasted vegetables. With each comforting spoonful, you can't help but smile, feeling the cozy embrace of winter and a deep craving for this delicious dish that will keep you satisfied all season long.

Preheat the oven to 400°F (200°C).

Rinse the farro thoroughly and cook per the package directions until the farro is tender. Once cooked, add 1 tablespoon (15 mL) olive oil and the parsley to the farro, mix well, cover, and set aside until ready to serve.

While the farro is cooking, place the butternut squash, zucchini, and Brussels sprouts on a baking sheet. Drizzle with 2 tablespoons (30 mL) olive oil and sprinkle with the thyme and herbes de Provence. Season with salt and pepper and mix well. Roast the vegetables for 25 to 30 minutes, until they are golden brown and the edges are slightly crispy. Set aside.

Make the dressing: In a blender or food processor, combine the basil, olive oil, nutritional yeast, mustard, lemon juice, parmesan, and balsamic vinegar. Blend the ingredients until the dressing reaches a smooth texture.

Place the arugula in a large bowl and drizzle with the remaining ½ tablespoon (7.5 mL) olive oil. Gently massage the arugula to coat evenly with the oil. Mix in the cooked farro and roasted vegetables. Drizzle the dressing over the mixture and toss to combine.

Serve in individual bowls, topped with pumpkin and sunflower seeds.

WHOLE ROASTED EGGPLANT WITH CREAMY TOFU

SERVES 2 TO 4　•　PREP TIME: 10 MINUTES　•　COOK TIME: 50 MINUTES

16 ounces (453 g) silken tofu

1 large eggplant

2 tablespoons (30 mL) sesame oil

1½ tablespoons (22.5 mL) tamari

1½ tablespoons (22.5 mL) maple syrup

1 tablespoon (15 mL) rice vinegar

½ teaspoon (2.5 mL) chili paste

1 teaspoon (5 mL) sesame seeds, toasted (see Note), for garnish

2 scallions, sliced, for garnish

We invite you to savor the smoky flavors of roasted eggplant paired with velvety tofu, capturing the simplicity and vibrancy of Mediterranean cuisine in every bite. This dish is the perfect centerpiece for a delicious meal.

Wrap the tofu in a few sheets of paper towels. Press between two plates for at least 15 minutes to soak up some of the excess liquid.

Preheat the oven to 375°F (190°C) and line a large baking pan with parchment paper.

Wash the eggplant and poke it a few times with a fork. Place on the prepared pan and roast in the oven for 50 minutes to 1 hour, until it feels cooked through and very soft. Allow the eggplant to cool for 10 minutes, then carefully remove the skin.

While the eggplant is in the oven, in a small bowl, whisk together the sesame oil, tamari, maple syrup, vinegar, and chili paste, and set aside.

Place the tofu in a medium bowl and whisk to a creamy consistency with a little texture. Spoon onto a shallow serving dish.

Slice the eggplant down the middle and place, cut side up, over the tofu, opening it up so the inside is exposed. Pour the tamari sauce over and garnish with the sesame seeds and scallions.

NOTE: *To toast the sesame seeds, spread them in a small skillet over medium heat. Cook, stirring occasionally, until they begin to turn golden brown, 3 to 4 minutes, keeping an eye on them as they can burn easily.*

ROASTED CAULIFLOWER WITH FRENCH-STYLE TABBOULEH AND HUMMUS

SERVES 2 · PREP TIME: 10 MINUTES · COOK TIME: 20 MINUTES

3 cups (750 mL) large cauliflower florets

2 tablespoons (30 mL) extra-virgin olive oil, divided

1 teaspoon (5 mL) herbes de Provence

kosher salt and freshly ground black pepper

½ cup (125 mL) whole wheat couscous

½ cup (125 mL) diced tomatoes

½ cup (125 mL) diced cucumber, seeds removed

2 cups (500 mL) firmly packed fresh curly leaf parsley

⅓ cup (80 mL) loosely packed fresh mint leaves

1 garlic clove

1 tablespoon (15 mL) onion powder

2 tablespoons (30 mL) freshly squeezed lemon juice

½ cup (125 mL) hummus

1 tablespoon (15 mL) za'atar

pita bread (optional)

CHLOÉ WRITES: The creation of this recipe was born of my profound love of French, Mediterranean, and Middle Eastern cuisine. As a foodie, I have always been captivated by the art of combining diverse culinary traditions. This dish is one of Trudy's favorites. She requests it whenever I visit her. The blend of flavors, spices, and freshness is everything she loves. Plus, it's quick and easy to make. It's perfect for us to cook and enjoy together.

Preheat the oven to 400°F (200°C).

On a large baking sheet, drizzle the cauliflower florets with 1 tablespoon (15 mL) olive oil. Sprinkle with the herbes de Provence and salt and pepper. Bake for about 20 minutes, or until the cauliflower turns golden and the edges are lightly crispy.

In a medium pot, combine the couscous and ½ cup (125 mL) water and bring to a boil over high heat. Turn off the heat, cover, and let sit until fluffy, about 5 minutes.

Press the tomatoes and cucumber with a paper towel to remove any excess water. Set aside.

In a food processor, combine the parsley, mint, garlic, and onion powder and pulse a few times until finely chopped. ➤

◄◄ *Make the tabbouleh:* Combine the couscous, tomatoes, cucumber, and parsley and mint mixture in a medium bowl. Add 1 tablespoon (15 mL) olive oil and the lemon juice, season with salt and pepper to taste, and mix.

On each plate, smear ¼ cup (60 mL) hummus in a circle. Top with the tabbouleh and then the roasted cauliflower. Sprinkle each with ½ tablespoon (7.5 mL) za'atar.

Serve with pita bread, if using.

STRAWBERRY AND CREAM CAKE

MAKES 1 CAKE • PREP TIME: 20 MINUTES • COOK TIME: 40 MINUTES

2 cups (500 mL) all-purpose flour

1 cup (250 mL) coconut sugar

½ teaspoon (2.5 mL) baking powder

½ teaspoon (2.5 mL) baking soda

⅓ cup (80 mL) avocado oil,
      plus 1 tablespoon for greasing the pan

1 tablespoon (15 mL) distilled white vinegar

2 teaspoons (10 mL) vanilla extract

¾ cup (180 mL) strawberry jam

2 cups (500 mL) vegan coconut whipped cream,
      store-bought or homemade (see Note), divided

2 cups (500 mL) fresh hulled and sliced strawberries

NOTE: *To make homemade coconut whipped cream, use one 14-ounce (400 ml) can unsweetened coconut cream. Add 2 to 3 tablespoons confectioners' sugar and whip for 3 to 4 minutes. Add 2 to 3 more tablespoons confectioners' sugar, depending on the sweetness you like, and whip again for 2 minutes.*

As the summer solstice graces us with its radiant presence, bringing long days and warm sunshine, it's time to savor the simple joys of the season. And what better way to celebrate than with a special treat like this strawberry and cream cake? Juicy red strawberries nestled in a cloud of creamy goodness form a heavenly dessert that embodies the essence of summer's magic.

Preheat the oven to 350°F (180°C) and grease a loaf or 9-inch round cake pan with 1 tablespoon avocado oil.

In a large bowl, whisk together the flour, coconut sugar, baking powder, and baking soda until well combined.

In another bowl, combine 1 cup (250 mL) cool water, ⅓ cup (80 mL) avocado oil, the vinegar, and vanilla and stir to mix. Add the wet ingredients to the dry ingredients and gently stir until there are no lumps.

Pour the batter into the prepared pan and bake for 35 to 40 minutes, until a toothpick inserted into the middle comes out clean.

Remove from the oven and let cool completely in the pan, about 20 minutes. Once cooled, remove the cake from the pan and cut in half horizontally.

On the bottom half of the cake, spread the strawberry jam in a thick layer, making sure to leave a half-inch border around the edge because the fillings will spread when the layers are sandwiched together. Spread 1 cup (250 mL) coconut whipped cream over the jam, again leaving a border.

Place the other cake half on top and spread with the remaining 1 cup (250 mL) coconut whipped cream. Layer the strawberries on top and serve.

DECADENT DOUBLE DARK CHOCOLATE COOKIES

MAKES 18 TO 20 · PREP TIME: 10 MINUTES · COOK TIME: 12 MINUTES

2½ cups (625 mL) all-purpose flour

1 cup (250 mL) packed light brown sugar

3 tablespoons (45 mL) dark cocoa powder

1 teaspoon (5 mL) baking powder

1 teaspoon (5 mL) baking soda

½ cup (125 mL) almond milk, at room temperature

½ cup (125 mL) melted vegan butter

3 tablespoons (45 mL) maple syrup

2 teaspoons (10 mL) vanilla extract

1 flax egg: 1 tablespoon (15 mL) flaxseed meal stirred into 2 tablespoons (30 mL) warm water

3.5 ounces (100 g) 70% dark chocolate

CHLOÉ WRITES: I'm a cookie person; I just love any type. But when I decided to make a double dark chocolate cookie, that's when I knew I had found my new favorite. They are soft, moist, and rich in flavor, and you'll always want to reach for another (sorry, not sorry).

Preheat the oven to 350°F (180°C) and line a large baking sheet with parchment paper.

In a large bowl, combine the flour, sugar, cocoa powder, baking powder, and baking soda. Mix well.

In a medium bowl, combine the almond milk, vegan butter, maple syrup, vanilla, and flax egg. Stir well.

Add the wet ingredients to the dry ingredients and stir until combined.

Roughly chop the chocolate into chunks, add to the cookie dough, and combine. Using a 1½-inch scoop or a generous tablespoon, scoop the cookie dough onto the prepared baking sheet; make sure the cookies are all uniform and are 1 to 2 inches apart.

Bake for about 12 minutes, or until the chocolate is melted. Once baked, transfer the cookies to a wire rack and let cool for 5 to 10 minutes. Serve warm.

STORAGE: *You can store the cookies in an airtight container for 3 or 4 days and in the freezer for up to a month.*

TRUDY WRITES: When Chloé was growing up, we spent many weekends with our best friends, who had a son around the same age. Both being only children, they became inseparable, like true brother and sister. We spent countless weekends in the city and memorable holidays on the beautiful beaches of Maine together. We swam happily in the cold ocean waters and savored the most delicious meals. Our shared love of cooking transformed each evening into a celebration that sparked our collective passion for food. Our friends' enthusiasm for creating magic at the table was as joyful and intense as ours!

In those shared moments, we created traditions that hold a profound significance in our lives. These memories influenced our past and shaped our future. Among them, the act of gathering with friends for a meal stands out as a moment of great joy. Whether it was an intimate dinner with a few or a lively gathering of many, whether we sat down formally or embraced the casual potluck spirit, those occasions left a mark in our hearts and on our lives.

The recipes in this chapter hold the power to foster connections and create new traditions when shared with others. The true beauty lies not in the flavors that we have put together but in the company they are shared with and the potential to inspire new rituals.

ROASTED CABBAGE WITH LEMON-TAHINI DRIZZLE, SCALLIONS, LIME CASHEWS, AND POMEGRANATE SEEDS

MAKES 6 WEDGES • PREP TIME: 15 MINUTES • COOK TIME: 45 MINUTES

FOR THE LIME CASHEWS

grated zest of 1 lime

½ teaspoon (2.5 mL) nutritional yeast

½ teaspoon (2.5 mL) kosher salt

½ teaspoon (2.5 mL) smoked paprika

¼ teaspoon (1.25 mL) cayenne pepper

freshly ground black pepper

½ tablespoon (7.5 mL) freshly squeezed lime juice

1 teaspoon (5 mL) avocado oil
   or other neutral-flavored oil such as canola

½ cup (125 mL) raw cashews

FOR THE CABBAGE

½ medium green cabbage, cut into 6 wedges

1 teaspoon (5 mL) ground coriander

½ teaspoon (2.5 mL) ground cumin

½ teaspoon (2.5 mL) turmeric powder

½ teaspoon (2.5 mL) garlic powder

½ teaspoon (2.5 mL) onion powder

½ teaspoon (2.5 mL) kosher salt

freshly ground black pepper

3 tablespoons (45 mL) extra-virgin olive oil

⅓ cup (80 mL) pomegranate seeds

2 scallions, thinly sliced on the diagonal, for garnish

FOR THE TAHINI SAUCE

½ cup (125 mL) tahini

¼ cup (60 mL) freshly squeezed lemon juice

1 garlic clove, finely grated

½ teaspoon (2.5 mL) kosher salt

1 tablespoon (15 mL) finely chopped fresh cilantro

1 tablespoon (15 mL) finely chopped fresh
   Italian parsley

TRUDY WRITES: This versatile side pairs perfectly with tofu or another vegetable entrée. I have a deep appreciation of cabbage and frequently incorporate it into meals. The first time I made this dish, I loved how well it paired with the creamy tahini sauce. It quickly became my go-to accompaniment that effortlessly complements any main course.

Preheat the oven to 350°F (180°C) and line two sheet pans with parchment paper.

Make the lime cashews: In a small bowl, combine the lime zest and nutritional yeast and set aside.

In another small bowl, combine the salt, paprika, cayenne, a few grinds of black pepper, the lime juice, avocado oil, and cashews and toss to coat the cashews well. Place the spiced nuts on one prepared sheet pan and roast in the oven for 10 to 15 minutes, until golden brown. Remove from the oven and toss with the lime zest and nutritional yeast mixture.

Make the cabbage: Place the cabbage wedges on the second prepared sheet pan. In a small bowl, make a paste by mixing the coriander, cumin, turmeric, garlic powder, onion powder, salt, a few grinds of black pepper, and the olive oil. Brush the cabbage wedges with the paste. Roast in the oven for 25 to 30 minutes, or until tender and beginning to brown. ➤

◂◂ *Make the tahini sauce:* In a medium bowl, whisk together the tahini, lemon juice, garlic, and salt. It will begin to thicken. Slowly pour in ½ cup (125 mL) ice water, whisking continuously, until the sauce is a smooth, creamy consistency. Add the cilantro and parsley and mix.

Serve the cabbage wedges on a platter, drizzled with the tahini sauce and topped with the lime cashews, pomegranate seeds, and sliced scallions.

ROASTED BRUSSELS SPROUTS WITH APPLE, CRANBERRIES, AND PECANS

SERVES 8 • PREP TIME: 15 MINUTES • COOK TIME: 20 MINUTES

9 large Brussels sprouts, ends trimmed,
    outer leaves removed, and halved

½ cup (125 mL) roughly chopped red onion

1 cup (250 mL) raw pecans

¼ teaspoon (1.25 mL) kosher salt

1 teaspoon (5 mL) freshly ground black pepper

1 medium Honeycrisp apple, unpeeled, cubed

½ cup (125 mL) dried cranberries

FOR THE SAUCE

3 tablespoons (45 mL) extra-virgin olive oil

1 tablespoon (15 mL) maple syrup

1 tablespoon (15 mL) Dijon mustard

1 tablespoon (15 mL) balsamic glaze or reduction

1 tablespoon (15 mL) nutritional yeast

Transporting us straight to the holidays, this mouthwatering side dish is the perfect addition to any meal. We just love seeing people's faces light up every time we bring this to any occasion.

Preheat the oven or an air fryer to 400°F (200°C) and line a baking sheet with parchment paper.

Place the Brussels sprouts, onion, and pecans on the prepared baking sheet, sprinkle with the salt and pepper, and toss together.

Make the sauce: In a small bowl, combine the olive oil, maple syrup, mustard, balsamic glaze, and nutritional yeast and mix well. Pour the sauce over the Brussels sprouts mixture and toss together.

Place the Brussels sprouts mixture into the oven (or air fryer) and roast for about 20 minutes, or until the sprouts are cooked through and charred on both sides. Flip the sprouts 10 minutes into roasting for even cooking. Check the pecans and remove if already browned.

While the Brussels sprouts mixture is roasting, place the apple and cranberries in a large serving bowl and set aside. Once the sprouts are done, add the mixture to the apple and cranberries and toss together.

AUTUMN KALE SALAD
WITH SQUASH AND BUTTER BEANS

SERVES 4 TO 6 • PREP TIME: 15 MINUTES • COOK TIME: 30 MINUTES

½ kabocha squash, peeled, seeds removed, and sliced into wedges

2 tablespoons (30 mL) olive oil, divided

2 teaspoons (10 mL) herbes de Provence, divided

one 15.5-ounce (439 g) can butter beans, drained and rinsed

1 bunch kale (8 to 10 stems)

1 large red onion, thinly sliced

¼ cup (60 mL) pumpkin seeds

1 tablespoon (15 mL) hemp hearts

⅓ cup (80 mL) crumbled vegan feta

⅓ cup (80 mL) dried cranberries

½ ripe avocado, thinly sliced

kosher salt and freshly ground black pepper

FOR THE DRESSING

2 tablespoons (30 mL) extra-virgin olive oil

2 tablespoons (30 mL) freshly squeezed lemon juice

1 tablespoon (15 mL) Dijon mustard

1 tablespoon (15 mL) nutritional yeast

2 teaspoons (10 mL) maple syrup

1 tablespoon (15 mL) balsamic vinegar

This warm, comforting salad brings together a medley of fresh, seasonal ingredients that showcase the vibrant colors and flavors of the fall. More than just a salad, this is a delicious and beautiful meal that we love to serve when we have a group of friends or family over.

Preheat the oven to 400°F (200°C) and line two medium baking sheets with parchment paper.

Place the kabocha squash wedges on one prepared baking sheet and coat them with 1 tablespoon (15 mL) olive oil and 1 teaspoon (5 mL) herbes de Provence. Toss to evenly distribute the seasonings. Roast in the oven for 25 to 30 minutes, until the squash is lightly browned.

On the other baking sheet, spread the butter beans and coat them with the remaining 1 tablespoon (15 mL) olive oil and 1 teaspoon (5 mL) herbes de Provence. Roast in the oven for about 20 minutes, or until crisp.

Rinse the kale and remove the leaves from the stems by squeezing each stem and slowly moving your hand down the leafy part. Discard the stems. Finely chop the kale and place into a large bowl.

Once the squash and butter beans are roasted, add them to the bowl with the kale along with the onion, pumpkin seeds, hemp hearts, vegan feta, dried cranberries, and avocado. Season with salt and pepper to taste. ➤➤

➤➤ *Make the dressing:* In a small bowl, whisk together the olive oil, lemon juice, mustard, nutritional yeast, maple syrup, and balsamic vinegar.

Pour the dressing over the salad and toss well to ensure that everything is evenly coated with the dressing.

NOTE: *You can adjust the seasoning and dressing according to your taste preferences.*

BOW TIE PASTA SALAD WITH KALE AND SUN-DRIED TOMATO DRESSING

SERVES 6 TO 8 • PREP TIME: 15 MINUTES • COOK TIME: 30 MINUTES

CHLOÉ WRITES: I remember the first time I took this bow tie pasta salad to a dinner with friends. The room was filled with laughter and joy as we gathered around the table to serve ourselves. Everyone was cracking jokes, and suddenly the room went silent when everyone started eating. Between moans and yums, we couldn't help but exchange glances of pure delight. The vibrant colors of the salad mirrored the vibrant energy in the room, and it seemed as though each ingredient had its own moment to shine. The conversation resumed, but now accompanied by the occasional compliment and request for the recipe. I hope you get to take this dish to a gathering with friends and have the same experience.

1 large red bell pepper, seeded and cut into 1-inch pieces

1 large orange bell pepper, seeded and cut into 1-inch pieces

½ cup (125 mL) red onion, cut into 1-inch pieces

3 tablespoons (45 mL) olive oil, divided

kosher salt and freshly ground black pepper

1 bunch cavolo nero kale

one 16-ounce (454 g) box bow tie pasta

2½ cups (625 mL) cherry tomatoes, halved

handful of fresh basil leaves

freshly grated vegan parmesan

FOR THE DRESSING

3 tablespoons (45 mL) olive tapenade

3 tablespoons (45 mL) balsamic vinegar

6 tablespoons (90 mL) extra-virgin olive oil

6 sun-dried tomatoes

1 garlic clove, finely grated

handful of fresh basil leaves

kosher salt and freshly ground black pepper

Preheat the oven to 375°F (190°C) and put a large pot of salted water on to boil.

In a large bowl, toss the red and orange bell peppers and onion with 1 tablespoon (15 mL) olive oil and season with salt and pepper. Spread the peppers and onion evenly on a sheet pan and cook in the oven for about 30 minutes, or until tender and beginning to brown.

Rinse the kale and remove the leaves from the stems by squeezing the stem and slowly moving your hand down the leafy part. Discard the stems. Slice the leaves into 1-inch strips. In another large bowl, toss the kale with 1 tablespoon (15 mL) olive oil, season with salt and pepper, turn out onto another sheet pan, and bake in the oven for about 20 minutes, or until it softens and wilts.

Make the dressing: Using a high-speed blender, combine the olive tapenade, balsamic vinegar, olive oil, sun-dried tomatoes, garlic, basil, a pinch of salt, and a few grinds of black pepper. Set aside. ➻

➻ Cook the pasta according to the package directions and drain.

In a large mixing bowl, toss the cooked pasta with the remaining 1 tablespoon (15 mL) olive oil. Add the veggies to the bowl along with the cherry tomatoes, basil leaves, and dressing. Toss well to combine and serve at room temperature with the parmesan.

STUFFED PACCHERI

SERVES 6 TO 8 • PREP TIME: 30 MINUTES • COOK TIME: 15 MINUTES

one 12-ounce (340 g) box paccheri

1 tablespoon (15 mL) extra-virgin olive oil

3 cups (750 mL) ground vegan "meat," thawed
(I use 4 Impossible burgers broken down
into small ground "beef" pieces)

2 teaspoons (10 mL) Italian seasoning

2 teaspoons (10 mL) garlic powder

1 teaspoon (5 mL) dried basil

½ teaspoon (2.5 mL) kosher salt

1 teaspoon (5 mL) freshly ground black pepper

2 cups (500 mL) roughly chopped fresh spinach

4 cups (1 L) store-bought vegan marinara sauce,
divided

2 cups (500 mL) shredded vegan cheese or mozzarella

CHLOÉ WRITES: When I first went plant-based, I was tired of making the same meals every day. I started testing a variety of hearty meals that would be both satisfying and flavorful. This recipe emerged as the perfect transitional dish and was the one that made my mom turn to a vegan diet. It is a crowd-pleaser for herbivores and carnivores alike. I don't doubt that it might become a weekly recipe in your household, too.

———————————————

Preheat the oven to 375°F (190°C).

Bring a large pot of salted water to a boil and cook the pasta until al dente, 1 to 2 minutes less than the time indicated on the package.

While your oven is heating and the pasta is boiling, add to a medium pan the olive oil and vegan ground "meat." Cook, stirring and breaking it up, until browned, about 5 minutes. Add the Italian seasoning, garlic powder, dried basil, salt, and pepper to the "meat" and combine. Add the spinach to the pan and cook, stirring occasionally to combine the flavors, until softened, about 2 minutes.

In a springform cake pan or a 9-inch round ovenproof glass dish with high sides, spread 1 cup (250 mL) marinara sauce evenly to cover the bottom.

Once the paccheri are al dente, drain the water, and do not rinse the pasta.

Stuff each pacchero with about 1½ tablespoons (22.5 mL) of the vegan "meat" mixture. Place the pasta upright in the pan, starting from the edge and working inward until it is full. Spread the remaining 3 cups (750 mL) marinara sauce on top of the paccheri and sprinkle evenly with the vegan cheese. ➟

◄◄ Bake for 10 minutes at 375°F (190°C), then switch to high broil for 5 minutes, keeping an eye on the pasta to make sure the cheese doesn't burn. (Vegan cheese doesn't really melt, so when it starts to bubble, you'll know it's done.)

Once done, allow to cool in the pan for at least 30 minutes, then remove the side of the springform pan and serve.

LENTIL AND VEGGIE SHEPHERD'S PIE WITH SWEET POTATO TOPPING

SERVES 8 TO 10 • COOK TIME: 45 MINUTES
PREP TIME: 25 MINUTES, PLUS OVERNIGHT SOAKING TIME FOR THE LENTILS

½ cup (125 mL) dried lentils

2 tablespoons (30 mL) extra-virgin olive oil,
    plus more for greasing the pan

1 large sweet potato

1 large white potato

½ large red onion, diced

2 garlic cloves, thinly sliced

2 bay leaves

1 fresh rosemary sprig

dried thyme

½ large carrot, diced

½ large celery stalk, diced

1 portobello mushroom, roughly chopped

1 tablespoon (15 mL) tomato paste

1 large tomato, grated

2½ cups (625 mL) vegetable broth

½ teaspoon (2.5 mL) kosher salt, plus more to taste

freshly ground black pepper

½ cup (125 mL) unsweetened almond milk

1 tablespoon (15 mL) vegan butter

1 tablespoon (15 mL) nutritional yeast

1 teaspoon (5 mL) fresh rosemary leaves, for garnish

crusty bread, for serving

CHLOÉ WRITES: This is such a classic, but it never fails. For me it is a winter dish, especially coming from Montreal, where the winters are cold and long. This comforting blend of sweet potato and lentils brings back memories of the *pâté chinois* (Quebec-style shepherd's pie) we used to have when I was a child. Just like those cherished meals, this combination provides a warm, satisfying experience, perfect for warding off the winter chill.

Cover the lentils with water and soak overnight or for at least a few hours.

Preheat the oven to 400°F (200°C) and grease a large ovenproof skillet, ovenproof glass dish, or pie dish with olive oil.

Wash the potatoes and poke with a fork a few times. Wrap them in foil and bake in the oven for about 40 minutes, or until soft. Set aside to cool until they can be handled.

In a medium cast-iron skillet or heavy-bottomed pan, heat the olive oil over medium heat, add the onion, and cook, stirring, until softened, 3 to 4 minutes. Add the garlic, bay leaves, rosemary, and a pinch of thyme and cook, stirring, for another 1 to 2 minutes. Add the carrot, celery, and mushroom and cook, stirring frequently, until the vegetables have softened, about 5 minutes. Stir in the tomato paste and cook for another 1 to 2 minutes. Add the lentils, tomato, and vegetable broth and stir to combine. Season with ½ teaspoon (2.5 mL) salt and a few grinds of pepper, and simmer, stirring frequently, until the liquid is reduced, 20 to 25 minutes. ➼

◄◄ *Make the potato crust:* Scoop out the flesh of the potatoes into a medium bowl. Mash with a fork until creamy, season with salt and pepper to taste, and add the almond milk, vegan butter, and nutritional yeast. Fill the prepared skillet three-quarters of the way with the lentil and vegetable mixture, and top with the potatoes. Bake for about 30 minutes, or until the top starts to brown.

Sprinkle with the rosemary leaves and serve with crusty bread.

CABBAGE, BEET, AND RADICCHIO COLESLAW WITH APPLE AND PLUMS

SERVES 4 TO 6 • PREP TIME: 20 MINUTES

2 cups (500 mL) thinly sliced cabbage

1 cup (250 mL) cubed canned or fresh beets (see Note)

1 cup (250 mL) thinly sliced radicchio

1 apple, unpeeled, sliced into thin wedges

2 plums, sliced into thin wedges

⅓ cup (80 mL) thinly sliced scallion, for garnish

1 tablespoon (15 mL) roughly chopped fresh chives, for garnish

⅓ cup (80 mL) pomegranate seeds, for garnish

FOR THE DRESSING

3 tablespoons (45 mL) extra-virgin olive oil

1 tablespoon (15 mL) nutritional yeast

1 tablespoon (15 mL) freshly squeezed lemon juice

½ tablespoon (7.5 mL) apple cider vinegar

1 tablespoon (15 mL) Dijon mustard

This colorful, refreshing salad is a feast for the eyes and taste buds. With its crunchy radicchio, earthy beets, sweet apple, and juicy plums, it's a vibrant, satisfying dish that anyone can enjoy. These simple ingredients come together to create a beautiful fresh coleslaw like no other.

Place the cabbage, beets, radicchio, apple, and plums in a large bowl and toss.

Make the dressing: To a small bowl, add the olive oil, nutritional yeast, lemon juice, vinegar, and mustard and mix well to combine.

Pour the dressing over the slaw and toss well. Serve on individual plates and top with the scallion, chives, and pomegranate seeds.

NOTE: *If using fresh beets, cook them for about 30 minutes in boiling water until they are easily pierced with a knife. Let cool completely, then peel.*

MUSHROOMS EN CROÛTE

SERVES 6 TO 8 • PREP TIME: 20 MINUTES • COOK TIME: 45 MINUTES

2 tablespoons (30 mL) extra-virgin olive oil,
    plus more for the baking sheet

one 14-ounce (397 g) vegan puff pastry sheet

1 cup (250 mL) chopped yellow onion

½ cup (125 mL) sliced celery stalks

½ cup (125 mL) peeled, diced carrots

4 cups (1 L) chopped cremini mushrooms

2 teaspoons (10 mL) cornstarch

2 teaspoons (10 mL) garlic powder

2 teaspoons (10 mL) herbes de Provence

one 15.5-ounce (439 g) can cooked lentils,
    drained and rinsed

1 tablespoon (15 mL) Dijon mustard

1 cup (250 mL) chopped fresh Italian parsley,
    plus more for garnish

kosher salt and freshly ground black pepper

CHLOÉ WRITES: This is the perfect meal for a holiday dinner with friends! This savory dish combines the earthy flavors of mushrooms with the comforting warmth of flaky pastry. Whenever I cook this dish, it brings back memories of laughter and joy from past celebrations, making it truly special and unforgettable.

Preheat the oven to 375°F (190°C) and oil a baking sheet. Remove the pastry dough from the freezer 30 minutes before baking.

In a large frying pan, heat 2 tablespoons (30 mL) olive oil over medium heat. Add the onion and cook, stirring, until caramelized and soft, about 10 minutes. Add the celery and carrots and cook, stirring, until softened, about 5 minutes. Add the mushrooms and cook, stirring, until softened, 6 to 8 minutes.

Once the vegetables are cooked, add the cornstarch, garlic powder, and herbes de Provence and stir together. Finally, add the lentils, mustard, and parsley and season with salt and pepper to taste, stirring constantly.

Place the puff pastry on the prepared baking sheet and spread the mixture on top. Fold the puff pastry to form a log.

Bake for about 45 minutes, or until the pastry is evenly cooked and golden. Check after 30 minutes. Remove from the oven and let cool for 10 minutes before serving.

RICOTTA AND SQUASH GALETTE

SERVES 2 TO 4 • PREP TIME: 15 MINUTES • COOK TIME: 30 MINUTES

neutral-flavored oil for the baking sheet

one 14-ounce (397 g) vegan puff pastry sheet

¾ cup (180 mL) vegan ricotta

½ white onion, thinly sliced

½ medium butternut squash, peeled, seeds removed, and sliced into ⅛-inch half moons

1 medium green zucchini or summer squash, sliced into ⅛-inch rounds

1 shallot, thinly sliced

1 teaspoon (5 mL) flaky sea salt, for topping

½ teaspoon (2.5 mL) freshly ground black pepper, for topping

⅓ cup (80 mL) sliced scallions, for topping

FOR THE SAUCE

1 tablespoon (15 mL) extra-virgin olive oil

1 tablespoon (15 mL) freshly squeezed lemon juice

1 tablespoon (15 mL) tahini

This rustic, savory galette embodies the essence of fall, evoking warm memories of spending crisp autumn days outside, gathering colorful leaves, and enjoying comforting meals with your friends and family, making it an ideal dish for embracing the season's cozy feeling.

Preheat the oven to 400°F (200°C) and oil a baking sheet and set aside. Remove the pastry dough from the freezer 30 minutes before baking.

Roll the pastry sheet into a circle about 12 inches in diameter. Transfer to the prepared baking sheet. Spread the vegan ricotta evenly over the dough, leaving about a half-inch border. Add the veggies and arrange in an even layer, starting with the onion, followed by the butternut squash, zucchini, and shallot. Gently fold the edges of the puff pastry over the filling, creating a rustic galette shape. Press the edges lightly to seal.

Bake for about 30 minutes, or until the crust is golden brown.

Make the sauce: In a small bowl, combine the olive oil, lemon juice, and tahini. Mix well.

When ready to serve, drizzle the galette with the lemon-tahini sauce and top with the salt, pepper, and scallions.

SPICY CORN RIBS
WITH CILANTRO-LIME DRIZZLE

MAKES 8 · PREP TIME: 5 MINUTES · COOK TIME: 25 MINUTES

2 ears fresh corn, husked

½ teaspoon (2.5 mL) ground cumin

½ teaspoon (2.5 mL) smoked paprika

¼ teaspoon (1.25 mL) kosher salt

cayenne pepper

freshly ground black pepper

3 tablespoons (45 mL) extra-virgin olive oil

1 teaspoon (5 mL) nutritional yeast

FOR THE CILANTRO-LIME DRIZZLE

⅓ cup (80 mL) very finely chopped cilantro leaves

2 tablespoons (30 mL) freshly squeezed lime juice

3 tablespoons (45 mL) extra-virgin olive oil

1 teaspoon (5 mL) maple syrup

1 garlic clove, finely grated

kosher salt

Spicy corn ribs with cilantro-lime drizzle is a mouthwatering dish that celebrates the flavors of fresh corn in a unique and delightful way. The corn is made into "ribs" by cutting them lengthwise and brushing them with a blend of spices that add a fiery kick. Roasted to perfection, they are then drizzled with a zesty cilantro-lime sauce that balances the heat with refreshing citrusy notes. It's the ultimate dish to enjoy on a warm summer evening with your friends, savoring the flavors of the season and creating unforgettable moments together.

Preheat the oven to 375°F (190°C) and line a baking pan with parchment paper.

Bring a medium pot of salted water large enough to fit the corn to a boil over high heat. Once the water is boiling, add the corn, reduce the heat to medium, and simmer for 5 minutes.

In a small bowl, mix the cumin, paprika, salt, a pinch of cayenne, a few grinds of black pepper, the olive oil, and nutritional yeast to make a paste.

Drain and rinse the corn ears under cold water until they are cool enough to handle. Cut each ear into 4 equal pieces, standing it up and slicing down the middle very slowly and carefully; you should have 8 corn ribs. Place the ribs on the prepared baking pan and brush them with the spice paste. Bake for about 20 minutes, turning halfway through, until they start to curl and crisp up.

Make the cilantro-lime drizzle: In a medium bowl, whisk together the cilantro, lime juice, olive oil, maple syrup, garlic, and a pinch of salt.

Remove the ribs from the oven, brush with the cilantro-lime drizzle, and serve.

RIGATONI BAKE
WITH ARTICHOKES, PEAS, AND SPINACH

SERVES 8 TO 10 • PREP TIME: 30 MINUTES • COOK TIME: 1 HOUR

one 16-ounce (453 g) box rigatoni

4 large garlic cloves, skin on

2½ cups (625 mL) unsweetened plant milk,
    such as almond or oat, divided

½ cup (125 mL) raw cashews,
    soaked in boiled water for at least 30 minutes

2 tablespoons (30 mL) nutritional yeast

½ teaspoon (2.5 mL) kosher salt

ground nutmeg

freshly ground black pepper

3 tablespoons (45 mL) extra-virgin olive oil

3 tablespoons (45 mL) all-purpose flour

one 12-ounce (340 g) jar marinated artichokes,
    drained and roughly chopped

2 large handfuls baby spinach

¼ cup (60 mL) frozen or fresh peas

grated zest of 1 lemon

½ cup (125 mL) grated vegan mozzarella

TRUDY WRITES: Our gatherings with friends often take the form of a potluck dinner. Each person contributes a dish they love, ranging from salads and pastas to appetizers and desserts. When it's my turn to provide a main dish, I bring this recipe, which is not only easy to make but also a guaranteed crowd-pleaser. Our evening begins with a lively apéro, followed by a delightful dinner and dessert with an array of delicious dishes. As the night progresses, it inevitably transforms into a dance party, creating unforgettable memories.

Preheat the oven to 350°F (180°C).

Cook the pasta until al dente per the package directions. Place the garlic cloves on a sheet pan and roast until soft, 20 to 25 minutes. Let cool and peel.

To a high-speed blender, add ½ cup (125 mL) plant milk, the cashews, nutritional yeast, salt, a large pinch of nutmeg, a grind of black pepper, and the garlic. Blend well until very smooth.

In a heavy-bottomed medium pan, heat the olive oil over medium heat. When it starts to shimmer, sift in the flour and whisk to combine for about 2 minutes, then add the remaining 2 cups (500 mL) plant milk, whisking constantly as the mixture thickens. Add the cashew mixture and continue whisking for another 5 minutes. The sauce should be thick and creamy. Remove from the heat.

Put the artichokes, spinach, peas, lemon zest, pasta, and white sauce into a large bowl and toss well to combine.

Transfer the pasta mixture to a large casserole dish and top with the vegan mozzarella. Cover with foil and bake for 20 minutes. Remove the foil and bake for an additional 15 minutes, until the top browns. To crisp the top and melt the vegan cheese, put the oven on broil for the last 1 to 2 minutes.

RAINBOW SUMMER BEET SALAD

SERVES 4 TO 6 • PREP TIME: 20 MINUTES • COOK TIME: 1 HOUR

4 medium fresh red beets

4 medium fresh golden beets

3 medium heirloom tomatoes

3 tablespoons (45 mL) extra-virgin olive oil

1 tablespoon (15 mL) freshly squeezed lime juice

1 teaspoon (5 mL) flaky sea salt

¼ cup (60 mL) thinly sliced scallions, for topping

3 tablespoons (45 mL) roughly chopped Italian parsley, for topping

2 tablespoons (30 mL) dukkah, for garnish (see Note)

CHLOÉ WRITES: Cooking beets can be long and messy, I know. Although, I really believe that taking the time to create something beautiful and delicious is worth every moment spent in the kitchen. This salad is colorful and irresistible. When it comes together, it's truly rewarding. It's a treat not only for the palate but for the eyes as well.

Preheat the oven to 400°F (200°C).

Wash the beets thoroughly and trim off the tops and roots. Wrap each beet separately in aluminum foil, ensuring they are tightly wrapped to prevent leakage. Place the wrapped beets on a baking sheet and roast them in the oven for about 1 hour, or until they are tender when pierced with a fork. Remove from the oven and let sit until cool enough to handle. When they are cool, gently peel off the skin using a small knife. The skin should come off easily.

Slice the peeled beets and the tomatoes into ¾-inch wedges and place on a serving platter or individual plates.

In a small mixing bowl, combine the olive oil, lime juice, and salt. Whisk the dressing until it emulsifies to a smooth consistency, and pour over the tomatoes and beets. Sprinkle the scallions and parsley on top. Finally, garnish with the dukkah.

NOTE: *Dukkah is an Egyptian nut and spice blend. If it is unavailable at your local grocery store, you can create your own by toasting and grinding a mixture of nuts and seeds such as pistachios, sesame seeds, coriander, cumin, and black peppercorns. Adjust the proportions to suit your taste preferences.*

SUMMER APRICOT TART

SERVES 8 • PREP TIME: 25 MINUTES • COOK TIME: 45 MINUTES

8 to 10 fresh apricots, cut into wedges

1 cup (250 mL) packed light brown sugar

¼ cup (60 mL) all-purpose flour

1 tablespoon (15 mL) freshly squeezed lemon juice

½ teaspoon (2.5 mL) vanilla extract

¼ teaspoon (1.25 mL) ground cinnamon

1 unbaked store-bought pie crust

¼ cup (60 mL) roughly chopped pistachios,
    for garnish

TRUDY WRITES: Summers bring with them the juicy delight of ripe apricots, and there's no better way to savor their sweetness than in a delectable apricot tart. My family home had three large apricot trees in the backyard, and I would eagerly await the ripening of the plump, fragrant fruit when I was growing up. The magic of this recipe lies not only in its deliciousness but also in the joy it brings through the memories it evokes.

Preheat the oven to the temperature indicated on the pie crust package.

In a large mixing bowl, combine the apricots, brown sugar, flour, lemon juice, vanilla, and cinnamon. Gently stir until well mixed. Let sit for about 10 minutes to allow the flavors to meld.

Place the pie crust into a 9-inch pie dish, pressing it gently against the side and bottom of the dish. Add the apricots in an even layer and pour the liquid in the bowl over the slices. With aluminum foil, make a tent and place around the edges to prevent the crust from burning. Place the pie on a baking sheet to catch any potential drips. This will also make it easier to remove from the oven later.

Bake the apricot pie according to the pie crust package directions, or until the crust is golden brown and the filling is bubbly and thickened.

Once baked, remove the pie from the oven and let cool on a wire rack for at least 1 hour before serving. This will allow the filling to set. When ready to serve, garnish with the pistachios.

MAPLE PECAN COOKIES

MAKES 18 TO 20 • PREP TIME: 10 MINUTES • COOK TIME: 15 MINUTES

1 cup (250 mL) spelt flour

1 cup (250 mL) pecans,
   plus ⅓ cup (80 mL) for topping

1 cup (250 mL) rolled oats

kosher salt

½ cup (125 mL) rice bran oil

½ cup (125 mL) maple syrup

Whether you're a seasoned baker or just starting out, this recipe is a breeze to make, providing mouthwatering results that will have anyone who eats them begging for more. So grab your apron, and let's dive into these delicious cookies, which will surely become a favorite in your kitchen!

Preheat the oven to 360°F (185°C) and line a baking pan with parchment paper.

In a food processor, pulse the flour, 1 cup (250 mL) pecans, oats, and a pinch of salt until it is a grainy-looking meal.

Add the oil and maple syrup and pulse until a dough forms.

Roll a spoonful of the dough into a small ball between your palms and place on the prepared baking pan. Repeat until all the dough has been used. Flatten dough balls slightly by pressing a pecan into the top of each. Bake for about 15 minutes, or until the cookies begin to brown around the edges.

Remove the cookies from the oven and transfer to a wire rack. Let cool for 20 minutes.

STORAGE: *Store in an airtight container in the fridge for up to 10 days or freeze in an airtight freezer bag for up to a month.*

WEEKDAY FAVORITES

TRUDY WRITES: Growing up with few established traditions, I yearned to create enduring rituals that would resonate throughout my adult life and inspire my daughter to create her own. It was during our transition to a plant-based lifestyle that the act of making soup became one of those traditions. We both found ourselves increasingly drawn to doing so, dedicating Sunday nights to its preparation and knowing that it would be an easy, quick meal during the week.

Weeknight recipes call for simplicity, allowing us to enjoy a fresh, delicious dinner without sacrificing precious time. Using fresh ingredients, whether luscious red tomatoes, crunchy cauliflower, or beets that brighten the plate, both elevates the visual appeal and satisfies our cravings.

Why not embark on your own journey of creating rituals by making a favorite soup once a week? This can be an excellent starting point for anyone looking to gradually reduce their consumption of meat and fish while still enjoying delicious meals.

CHICKPEA, PASTA, AND VEGGIE SOUP

SERVES 8 TO 10 · PREP TIME: 35 MINUTES · COOK TIME: 33 MINUTES

2 tablespoons (30 mL) extra-virgin olive oil

1 cup (250 mL) chopped white onion

5 garlic cloves, minced

2 teaspoons (10 mL) dried thyme, divided

2 teaspoons (10 mL) Italian seasoning, divided

1¼ cups (310 mL) peeled, diced carrots

1 cup (250 mL) chopped celery stalks

2 tablespoons (30 mL) tomato paste

2 cups (500 mL) peeled, cubed butternut squash
  or sweet potato

9 cups (2.25 L) vegetable broth

3 cups (750 mL) hot water

one 14.5-ounce (411 g) can diced
  fire-roasted tomatoes

2¼ cups (560 mL) pasta, such as macaroni
  or small shells

one 15.5-ounce (439 g) can chickpeas,
  drained and rinsed

2 cups (500 mL) chopped lacinato (dinosaur) kale,
  stems removed

½ teaspoon (2.5 mL) flaky sea salt

1 teaspoon (5 mL) freshly cracked black pepper

vegan parmesan cheese, for serving (optional)

chopped parsley for garnish (optional)

CHLOÉ WRITES: This comforting bowl of goodness takes me back to my childhood. This simple soup brings back memories of coming home from school on frosty winter days. I used to love Campbell's minestrone. It was a fan favorite in our household, and I knew I could create something hearty that would recapture those special moments. To me, this classic dish is more than just a soup; it's a reminder of slower times and the power of nostalgia in food.

Heat the olive oil in a large pot with a lid over medium heat. When it starts to shimmer, add the onion and garlic and cook, stirring, until the onion becomes translucent, about 5 minutes. Add ½ teaspoon (2.5 mL) thyme and ½ teaspoon (2.5 mL) Italian seasoning and cook, stirring, for about 5 minutes more. Add the carrots, celery, and tomato paste and stir well until the tomato paste coats everything. Stir in the butternut squash. Add the vegetable broth, water, the tomatoes with their liquid, and the remaining thyme and Italian seasoning and bring to a boil. Reduce the heat to low, cover, and simmer until the carrots have softened, about 15 minutes.

Add the pasta and chickpeas and continue simmering until the pasta is al dente, 6 to 8 minutes. Remove the pot from the heat, add the kale, and stir to combine until the kale has wilted. Season with the salt and pepper.

Serve in bowls sprinkled with grated or shaved vegan parmesan and chopped parsley for extra flavor and goodness, if using.

CREAMY SWISS CHARD FETTUCCINE

SERVES 4 TO 6 • PREP TIME: 15 MINUTES • COOK TIME: 20 MINUTES

one 16-ounce (454 g) box fettuccine

2 tablespoons (30 mL) extra-virgin olive oil

2 tablespoons (30 mL) vegan butter

⅓ cup (80 mL) roughly chopped shallot

2 garlic cloves, minced

¼ cup (60 mL) dry white wine or vegetable broth

6 leaves Swiss chard, stems removed,
   roughly chopped

2 fresh rosemary sprigs

2 tablespoons (30 mL) fresh thyme leaves

1½ cups (375 mL) unsweetened vegan creamer

1 teaspoon (5 mL) truffle salt or kosher salt

1 teaspoon (5 mL) freshly ground black pepper

½ cup (125 mL) grated vegan parmesan, divided

CHLOÉ WRITES: One chilly December evening, as the snow-flakes softly fell outside, I found myself cozied up on the couch, watching one of my favorite movies, *The Holiday*. The scene where Cameron Diaz's character whips up a scrumptious fettuccine dish caught my attention, sparking inspiration to create my own version. And thus the creamy Swiss chard fettuccine was born, a dish that encapsulates the warmth, flavors, and enchantment of that memorable movie moment.

Bring a large pot of water to a boil. Cook the pasta until al dente according to the package directions.

Place the olive oil and butter in a large skillet over medium heat. When the butter has melted, add the shallot and garlic and cook, stirring, until the shallot has softened, 2 to 3 minutes. Add the wine and stir to deglaze the pan.

Add the Swiss chard, rosemary, and thyme and cook, stirring, until the chard starts to wilt, 5 to 6 minutes.

Stir in the vegan creamer and season with the salt and pepper. Remove the rosemary sprigs, add the cooked pasta and ¼ cup (60 mL) parmesan, and toss.

Serve and top with the remaining ¼ cup (60 mL) parmesan.

WARM SPICY FARRO WITH SHIITAKE MUSHROOMS AND GARLIC CRISPS

SERVES 4 · PREP TIME: 15 MINUTES · COOK TIME: 35 MINUTES

1¼ cups (310 mL) farro

6 tablespoons (90 mL) extra-virgin olive oil, divided

1 small butternut squash,
    peeled and cut in ½-inch cubes

kosher salt and freshly ground black pepper

3 large garlic cloves, thinly sliced

1 cup (250 mL) frozen peas

½ cup (125 mL) diced red onion

2 cups (500 mL) shiitake mushrooms,
    stems removed, roughly chopped

1 tablespoon (15 mL) chili oil

½ teaspoon (2.5 mL) truffle salt

2 teaspoons (10 mL) freshly ground black pepper

½ cup (125 mL) tzatziki (see page 178)

1 cup (250 mL) broccoli sprouts, for topping

1 avocado sliced into 8 wedges, for topping

This delectable dish brings together the comforting goodness of nutty farro grains, earthy shiitake mushrooms, and irresistible crispy garlic bites. With simple ingredients and straightforward steps, you'll be amazed at how effortlessly you can create a cozy, flavorful meal that will impress both you and your loved ones.

Preheat the oven to 400°F (200°C).

Rinse the farro and cook according to the package directions. Add 1 tablespoon (15 mL) olive oil to the cooked farro and stir well. Set aside, covered, until ready to plate.

Spread the butternut squash on a baking sheet, drizzle with 2 tablespoons (30 mL) olive oil, and season with salt and pepper. Roast, shaking the baking sheet halfway through, until the cubes are golden brown and tender, about 20 minutes. Let cool.

Heat the remaining 3 tablespoons (45 mL) olive oil in a large frying pan over high heat. Line a plate with a paper towel and set aside. When the oil starts to shimmer, add the garlic and fry, watching carefully because garlic burns easily, until the garlic starts to look like chips and is golden brown. Remove the garlic chips from the pan and set on the prepared plate to absorb any oil.

To the same pan, add the frozen peas and cook, stirring, for 1 to 2 minutes. Add the onion and mushrooms and cook, stirring frequently, until the onion has softened and the mushrooms are tender, another 4 to 5 minutes. Stir in the farro, garlic chips, chili oil, truffle salt, and pepper.

Serve the warm farro over the tzatziki, topped with the broccoli sprouts and avocado wedges.

TANGY LEMON PESTO PASTA

SERVES 4 TO 6 • PREP TIME: 10 MINUTES • COOK TIME: 10 MINUTES

one 16-ounce (454 g) box mafalda or trenette

3 cups (750 mL) packed fresh basil leaves

2 tablespoons (30 mL) nutritional yeast

2 tablespoons (30 mL) freshly squeezed lemon juice

¼ cup (60 mL) vegan parmesan, plus more for garnish

2 garlic cloves

½ teaspoon (2.5 mL) chili flakes

½ cup (125 mL) extra-virgin olive oil

kosher salt and freshly ground black pepper

We know this dish stirs up quite a controversy among foodies and traditionalists. Though some may gasp at the thought of squeezing a lemon into their beloved pesto, the ones who make it tend to never go back. This tangy twist turns it into the most mouthwatering pesto you will ever try.

Bring a large pot of water to a boil and cook the pasta until al dente per the package directions. Drain, reserving ½ cup (125 mL) of the pasta water.

To a food processor, add the basil, nutritional yeast, lemon juice, parmesan, garlic, chili flakes, and olive oil. Season with salt and pepper and pulse until smooth.

Transfer the pasta back to the pot, add the pesto, and toss to coat the pasta evenly. Add reserved pasta water as needed for the consistency you prefer. Garnish with parmesan and serve.

SHAWARMA SPICE TOFU SKEWERS WITH HUMMUS AND WILTED SPINACH

SERVES 2 • COOK TIME: 15 MINUTES

PREP TIME: 30 MINUTES, PLUS 1 TO 2 HOURS OR OVERNIGHT TO MARINATE

16 ounces (454 g) extra-firm tofu

3 tablespoons (45 mL) extra-virgin olive oil

2 tablespoons (30 mL) freshly squeezed lemon juice, plus more for serving

2 garlic cloves, minced

1 teaspoon (5 mL) maple syrup

1 teaspoon (5 mL) ground coriander

1 teaspoon (5 mL) smoked paprika

1 teaspoon (5 mL) ground cumin

¼ teaspoon (1.25 mL) ground cardamom

¼ teaspoon (1.25 mL) ground cinnamon

½ teaspoon (2.5 mL) ground ginger

½ teaspoon (2.5 mL) ground turmeric

¼ teaspoon (1.25 mL) chili flakes

¾ teaspoon (3.75 mL) kosher salt

freshly ground black pepper

1 tablespoon (15 mL) neutral-flavored oil, such as canola

3 cups (750 mL) baby spinach leaves

one 8-ounce (227 g) container hummus (see Note)

This is the perfect summer evening meal, whether savored with a friend or relished in your own company. However you choose to cook these delectable skewers—in a stovetop pan or on a barbecue to create a smoky essence—the flavors will transport you. There's something about the combination of charred tofu, creamy hummus, and wilted spinach that captures the essence of warm summer nights.

Wrap the tofu block in a kitchen towel, place it between two sheet pans, and put a heavy weight on top, such as a cast-iron skillet or a large can of beans. Press for at least 15 minutes. Once the excess moisture has been removed, cut the tofu into 1-inch cubes.

In a medium bowl, whisk together the olive oil, lemon juice, garlic, maple syrup, coriander, paprika, cumin, cardamom, cinnamon, ginger, turmeric, chili flakes, salt, and a few grinds of black pepper.

Add the tofu to the marinade, making sure it is completely submerged in the liquid. Place in the fridge, covered, for 1 to 2 hours, or overnight.

Remove the tofu from the fridge 30 minutes before cooking. Thread the tofu cubes onto 2 skewers (see Note). Reserve the remaining marinade.

Heat a large heavy-bottomed pan or cast-iron skillet over medium heat. Drizzle in the neutral-flavored oil. When it starts to shimmer, add the skewers and cook until golden brown, 2 to 3 minutes on each side. ➻

◄◄ Remove the skewers from the pan and wipe the pan with a paper towel. Add 3 tablespoons (45 mL) of the reserved marinade to the pan and heat for 30 seconds. Add the baby spinach and cook, stirring, until wilted, about 2 minutes.

Spoon the hummus onto a serving platter and top with the spinach. Place the tofu skewers on top and drizzle with more lemon juice.

NOTE: *The hummus can be the flavor of your choice. If using wooden skewers, soak in water for 30 minutes before cooking.*

SEARED GREEN BEANS
WITH TOFU MINCE

SERVES 4 · PREP TIME: 20 MINUTES · COOK TIME: 15 MINUTES

8 ounces (227 g) extra-firm tofu

4 tablespoons (60 mL) sesame oil, divided

3 tablespoons (45 mL) tamari

2 tablespoons (30 mL) unsweetened crunchy
    peanut butter

2 tablespoons (30 mL) tahini

½ teaspoon (2.5 mL) onion powder

½ teaspoon (2.5 mL) garlic powder

1 teaspoon (5 mL) smoked paprika

2 tablespoons (30 mL) nutritional yeast

kosher salt and freshly cracked black pepper

½ pound (453 g) fresh long green beans, trimmed

1 tablespoon (15 mL) toasted sesame seeds

This tofu mince is delicious, especially when served over seared beans. However, it also pairs wonderfully with asparagus or broccolini. Its light, delicate flavor enhances the taste of any vegetable it accompanies. This dish is not only incredibly tasty but also satisfying and filling. Plus, it's super easy to make, allowing you to enjoy a delicious weekday meal in just 35 minutes.

Wrap the tofu block in a kitchen towel, place it between two sheet pans, and put a heavy weight on top, such as a cast-iron skillet or canned beans. Press for at least 15 minutes. Once the excess moisture has been removed, crumble the tofu into small pieces with the back of a fork.

Preheat the oven to 400°F (200°C) and line a large sheet pan with parchment paper.

In a medium bowl, mix together 3 tablespoons (45 mL) sesame oil, the tamari, peanut butter, tahini, onion powder, garlic powder, paprika, nutritional yeast, and salt and pepper to taste. Add the tofu and toss until the tofu is coated with the mixture.

Place the tofu on the prepared sheet pan and bake for 20 to 25 minutes, until dark and crispy. Remove from the oven and set aside.

Bring a medium pot of salted water to a boil over high heat. Add the green beans to the pot and blanch until just tender, about 4 minutes, then drain and immediately rinse under cold water to stop the cooking process. Dry the beans completely using paper towels or a kitchen towel. ➤➤

↞ Heat the remaining 1 tablespoon (15 mL) sesame oil in a heavy-bottomed pan, wok, or cast-iron skillet over medium heat. When it starts to shimmer, add the blanched green beans to the pan. Season with additional salt and pepper to taste. Once the beans begin to blister and color, remove from the pan and place on a serving dish.

Spread the tofu mince over the green beans, sprinkle with the toasted sesame seeds, and serve.

NIÇOISE SALAD

SERVES 4 • PREP TIME: 30 MINUTES • COOK TIME: 30 MINUTES

10 fresh long green beans

12 baby potatoes, halved

¼ cup (60 mL) diced red onion

½ cup (125 mL) marinated artichokes,
    drained and roughly chopped

2 tablespoons (30 mL) capers, drained

3 gherkin pickles, sliced into discs

¼ cup (60 mL) roughly chopped kalamata olives

1 teaspoon (5 mL) kosher salt

1 teaspoon (5 mL) freshly ground black pepper

2 teaspoons (10 mL) herbes de Provence, for garnish

FOR THE DRESSING

1 tablespoon (15 mL) whole grain mustard

2 tablespoons (30 mL) extra-virgin olive oil

1 teaspoon (5 mL) freshly squeezed lemon juice

1 teaspoon (5 mL) minced garlic

2 teaspoons (10 mL) minced shallot

CHLOÉ WRITES: In this vegan version of the classic Niçoise salad, you won't miss the eggs or fish at all. I've enjoyed this salad numerous times, and to be honest, it surpasses my memories of the traditional version. It has a wonderful combination of flavors and textures that come together beautifully. It showcases the way plant-based ingredients can create an equally delicious, satisfying dish.

Bring a large pot of salted water to a boil over high heat. Add the green beans and blanch until they are vibrant green and firm, about 5 minutes. Using a spider or slotted spoon, remove the green beans and immediately rinse under cold water to stop the cooking process. Set aside to drain on a paper towel–lined plate. Place the potatoes into the same pot and boil until fork tender, 10 to 15 minutes. Drain on a paper towel–lined plate, then place into a large salad bowl.

Make the dressing: In a small bowl, whisk together the mustard, olive oil, lemon juice, garlic, and shallot until emulsified.

Slice the green beans in half lengthwise and add to the salad bowl along with the onion, artichokes, capers, pickles, olives, salt, and pepper, and toss with the dressing.

Serve in individual bowls, each garnished with ½ teaspoon (2.5 mL) herbes de Provence.

TARTINES TOPPED WITH SAVORY CASHEW CREAM, TOMATOES, AND MICROGREENS

SERVES 1 OR 2 • COOK TIME: 5 MINUTES • PREP TIME: 10 MINUTES, PLUS 30 MINUTES TO 1 HOUR OR OVERNIGHT TO SOAK THE CASHEWS

FOR THE CASHEW CREAM

½ cup (125 mL) raw cashews, soaked overnight or for at least 30 minutes to 1 hour

2 tablespoons (30 mL) nutritional yeast

1 teaspoon (5 mL) white miso paste

1 teaspoon (5 mL) extra-virgin olive oil

½ teaspoon (2.5 mL) flaky sea salt

freshly ground black pepper

FOR THE TARTINES

2 thick slices good sourdough bread

extra-virgin olive oil

1 heirloom tomato, sliced

flaky sea salt and freshly ground black pepper

¼ cup microgreens, for garnish

TRUDY SAYS: When I arrive home late from a busy day, this is the supper that I love to make. The key to making these tartines truly exceptional is using fresh, incredibly ripe tomatoes. Their juicy sweetness elevates the flavors to another level. To take them from simple sandwiches to delightful tartines, I add a dollop of creamy cashew cream. This type of recipe is an easy way to incorporate a plant-based meal into your day-to-day.

Make the cashew cream: To a high-speed blender, add the cashews, ¼ cup (60 mL) water, the nutritional yeast, miso paste, olive oil, salt, and a few grinds of pepper and blend until very smooth and creamy.

Make the tartines: Toast the bread. Drizzle the toasts with olive oil and spread half the cashew cream on each slice. Top each with half the tomato and another drizzle of olive oil. Sprinkle with flaky salt and a few grinds of pepper, and top with the microgreens.

CREAMY MUSHROOM RISOTTO

SERVES 6 • PREP TIME: 20 MINUTES • COOK TIME: 30 MINUTES

8 cups (2 L) vegetable broth

1 cup (250 mL) dried porcini mushrooms

2 fresh thyme sprigs, leaves only

2 tablespoons (30 mL) vegan butter

1 cup (250 mL) roughly chopped sweet onion

4 garlic cloves, minced

½ cup (125 mL) thinly sliced celery stalks

4 cups (1 L) sliced cremini mushrooms, stems removed

2 teaspoons (10 mL) Italian seasoning

1 teaspoon (5 mL) freshly ground black pepper

1 teaspoon (5 mL) kosher salt

2 tablespoons (30 mL) extra-virgin olive oil

2 cups (500 mL) Arborio rice

1 cup (250 mL) dry white wine
  (or substitute with extra vegetable broth)

¾ cup (180 mL) unsweetened vegan creamer

½ cup (125 mL) grated vegan parmesan,
  plus ¼ cup (60 mL) shaved vegan parmesan,
  for serving

⅓ cup (60 mL) roughly chopped fresh Italian parsley,
  divided

CHLOÉ SAYS: This recipe holds a special place in my heart. It is a cherished memory of a collaborative cooking experience with a dear friend of mine, Maria. As we stood side by side, sautéing the mushrooms and stirring the Arborio rice, we couldn't stop laughing and enjoying the process. When we finally sat down to our risotto-filled bowls and glasses of white wine, chatting about food, life, and our endless love of home cooking, we couldn't help but gush over the perfect combination of flavors and textures we had just created. I love cooking with friends because there's something truly magical that happens when we come together to make something special.

Place the broth, porcini mushrooms, and thyme leaves in a large pot and bring to a boil. Reduce the heat to medium-low and simmer for 15 minutes.

In a large skillet, melt the vegan butter over medium-high heat. Add the onion and cook, stirring, until softened, about 2 minutes. Add the garlic and celery and cook, stirring, until the vegetables become fragrant and translucent, 3 to 4 minutes. Add the cremini mushrooms, Italian seasoning, black pepper, salt, and olive oil and cook, stirring, until the mushrooms are soft, about 5 minutes more.

Add the rice and stir to combine with the vegetables. Pour in the wine, stirring continuously, until absorbed, about 5 minutes.

Ladle ½ cup (125 mL) of the mushroom broth into the rice and cook, stirring continuously, until the rice has absorbed the liquid, about 5 minutes. Repeat, adding ½ cup (125 mL) of the broth at a time, until the rice is al dente; the whole process should take 20 to 30 minutes (you may not need all of the broth). Add the mushrooms and thyme from the broth to the risotto. ➤➤

↤ Reduce the heat to low, add the vegan creamer, and stir for 1 minute, then add ½ cup (125 mL) grated parmesan and ¼ cup (80 mL) parsley and mix.

Serve in shallow bowls sprinkled with the remaining parsley and with the shaved parmesan on the side.

BEET AND STRAWBERRY SALAD WITH ARUGULA, QUINOA, TOASTED HAZELNUTS, AND APPLE CIDER VINAIGRETTE

SERVES 4 TO 6 · PREP TIME: 5 MINUTES · COOK TIME: 15 MINUTES

FOR THE APPLE CIDER VINAIGRETTE

½ tablespoon (7.5 mL) apple cider vinegar

2 tablespoons (30 mL) extra-virgin olive oil

1 teaspoon (5 mL) Dijon mustard

1 teaspoon (5 mL) maple syrup

1 garlic clove, chopped

kosher salt and freshly ground black pepper

FOR THE SALAD

1 cup (250 mL) cooked white quinoa

2 cups (500 mL) arugula

½ pint (237 g) strawberries, hulled and sliced

1 medium cooked beet, diced (see Note)

¼ cup (60 mL) roasted hazelnuts, chopped

¼ cup (60 mL) lightly packed microgreens, for garnish

TRUDY WRITES: This is the perfect summer salad. When I pass the local market on the way to the cottage, I often stop in for fresh-picked strawberries. They are always so sweet and are the greatest treat. Combining them with quinoa and beets makes an easy, delicious meal.

Make the vinaigrette: To a high-speed blender, add the vinegar, olive oil, mustard, maple syrup, garlic, and salt and pepper to taste and blend until smooth.

Make the salad: Place the quinoa, arugula, strawberries, beet, hazelnuts, and vinaigrette into a large bowl and toss to combine. Garnish with the microgreens.

NOTE: *If using raw beets, cook them for about 30 minutes in boiling water until easily pierced with a knife. Let cool completely, then peel.*

MISO-GLAZED EGGPLANT WITH HOMEMADE TZATZIKI

SERVES 2 • COOK TIME: 20 MINUTES
PREP TIME: 10 MINUTES, PLUS 1 HOUR FOR RESTING
AND 1 HOUR FOR MELDING

FOR THE TZATZIKI

2 Persian cucumbers

kosher salt

2 cups (500 mL) unsweetened plain vegan yogurt, such as cashew or almond

3 garlic cloves, minced

¼ cup (60 mL) chopped fresh dill

¼ cup (60 mL) chopped fresh mint

2 tablespoons (30 mL) freshly squeezed lemon juice

2 tablespoons (30 mL) extra-virgin olive oil

freshly ground black pepper

1 medium eggplant

extra-virgin olive oil

2 tablespoons (30 mL) miso paste

2 tablespoons (30 mL) tamari

2 tablespoons (30 mL) hoisin sauce

1 tablespoon (15 mL) maple syrup

2 teaspoons (10 mL) cornstarch

1 garlic clove, crushed

TOPPINGS

¼ cup (60 mL) pickled red onions (see Note)

⅓ cup (80 mL) microgreens

1 fresh red chile, diced

fresh mint leaves

baby arugula

TRUDY WRITES: I was never a fan of eggplant, but this recipe Chloé made miraculously transforms even the staunchest eggplant critics into avid fans. The magic lies in the harmonious marriage of the miso glaze, which imparts a depth of umami, and the eggplant's natural creaminess, resulting in a sublime texture that will leave you wanting more.

Make the tzatziki: Grate the cucumbers into a medium bowl and stir in a pinch of salt. Let rest for about 1 hour. After an hour, using a slotted spoon, transfer the cucumber to a clean kitchen towel and squeeze out the excess moisture. You can also place the cucumber in a fine-mesh strainer and press it with a spoon to remove the moisture. In a medium bowl, combine the yogurt, garlic, dill, mint, lemon juice, and olive oil. Add the cucumber to the yogurt mixture and mix well to combine. Season, starting with a pinch of salt and a grind of pepper, then adjust the flavor by adding more lemon juice, dill, mint, garlic, and/or salt to taste. Cover the bowl with plastic wrap and refrigerate for at least an hour before serving. This allows the flavors to meld.

Preheat the broiler on low and line a baking sheet with parchment paper.

Cut the eggplant in half lengthwise and score the cut sides with a knife in a crisscross pattern. Lightly coat the cut sides of the eggplant halves with olive oil. ➻

↤ Heat a medium pan over high heat and place the eggplant halves skin side down in the pan. Cook until the skin begins to brown, 5 to 6 minutes. Flip and cook until the cut side begins to brown, 3 to 4 minutes more.

Meanwhile, in a small bowl, whisk together the miso paste, tamari, hoisin sauce, maple syrup, cornstarch, and garlic to a smooth consistency.

Remove the eggplant halves from the pan and place on the prepared baking sheet with the cut sides up. Brush each piece generously with the miso glaze and broil for about 4 minutes, or until the glaze starts bubbling.

Smear half the tzatziki on each of two plates, then add the eggplant halves on top. Serve with the toppings alongside.

NOTE: *Pickled onions are so easy to make. In a small saucepan, combine ½ cup (125 mL) water, ½ cup (125 mL) distilled white vinegar, 2 tablespoons (30 mL) coconut sugar, 1 tablespoon (15 mL) black peppercorns, 1 tablespoon (15 mL) mustard seeds, and 1 tablespoon (15 mL) kosher salt. Simmer over low heat until the sugar and salt have dissolved. Set aside to cool. Thinly slice a large red onion, add to the liquid ingredients, and stir to combine. Place the onion and liquid into a jar with an airtight lid. Use after 3 hours, and store in the fridge for up to 2 weeks.*

SWEET POTATO AND ORZO SALAD

SERVES 4 TO 6 • PREP TIME: 10 MINUTES • COOK TIME: 25 MINUTES

4 small sweet potatoes,
  peeled and sliced in half lengthwise

3 tablespoons (45 mL) olive oil, divided

1 cup (250 mL) orzo

5 ounces (142 g) arugula

2 shallots, thinly sliced

1 Honeycrisp apple, cut into matchsticks

¼ cup (60 mL) roughly chopped unsalted walnuts

¼ cup (60 mL) dried cranberries

⅓ cup (80 mL) vegan feta, crumbled

2 tablespoons (30 mL) chopped fresh dill

kosher salt and freshly ground black pepper

FOR THE DRESSING

2½ tablespoons (37.5 mL) rosemary-infused olive oil
  or extra-virgin olive oil

1 tablespoon (15 mL) Dijon mustard

1 tablespoon (15 mL) balsamic vinegar

½ tablespoon (7.5 mL) nutritional yeast

This salad is the star any night of the week. It's a simple yet incredible dish in which tender roasted sweet potatoes and orzo come together in a delicious harmony. It's guaranteed to make anyone want a second serving, and maybe a third.

Preheat the oven to 400°F (200°C).

Coat the sweet potatoes with 1 tablespoon (15 mL) olive oil and place on a baking sheet. Roast for 15 to 20 minutes, until the sweet potatoes are cooked through.

Bring 4 cups (1 L) water to a boil in a large pot. Add the orzo and cook until al dente per the package directions. Drain and set aside.

In a large bowl, coat the arugula with the remaining 2 tablespoons (30 mL) olive oil.

On a large platter, top the sweet potatoes with the orzo, arugula, shallots, apple, walnuts, and cranberries. Sprinkle with the feta and dill and season with salt and pepper to taste.

Make the dressing: Whisk together the olive oil, mustard, balsamic vinegar, and nutritional yeast until emulsified. Drizzle the dressing over the salad.

PEANUT BUTTER FUDGE

MAKES 12 SQUARES • PREP TIME: 15 MINUTES, PLUS 2 HOURS TO CHILL

½ cup (125 mL) coconut oil

1 cup (250 mL) unsweetened smooth peanut butter

¼ cup (60 mL) maple syrup

1½ cups (375 mL) unsweetened shredded coconut

flaky sea salt

TRUDY WRITES: This recipe combines two of my favorite things, peanut butter and maple syrup! It's a wonderful treat for after dinner or as a midafternoon pick-me-up.

Line a loaf pan or 8-inch square cake pan with parchment paper, leaving a lip of parchment.

In a small pan, slightly warm the coconut oil over low heat so it is easier to blend. To a high-speed blender, add the coconut oil, peanut butter, maple syrup, shredded coconut, and a pinch of salt and blend until smooth, scraping the sides down a few times if needed.

Pour the mixture into the prepared pan, and place in the fridge to chill for at least 2 hours. When chilled, cut into 12 squares and enjoy.

STORAGE: *Keep in an airtight container in the fridge for up to 7 days.*

RUSTIC PEAR CRISP

SERVES 10 • PREP TIME: 20 MINUTES • COOK TIME: 40 TO 50 MINUTES

FOR THE FILLING

4 medium pears, cored and thinly sliced into wedges

juice of 1 lemon

2 tablespoons (30 mL) coconut sugar

2 teaspoons (10 mL) ground cinnamon

2 tablespoons (30 mL) cornstarch

FOR THE TOPPING

1¼ cups (310 mL) rolled oats

⅓ cup (80 mL) almond flour

⅓ cup (80 mL) all-purpose flour

½ cup (125 mL) coconut sugar

½ cup (125 mL) chopped toasted unsalted walnuts

2 teaspoons (10 mL) ground cinnamon

1 cup (250 mL) melted coconut oil

CHLOÉ WRITES: I'm an apple crisp lover, but I can promise you that pears bring this one to a whole other level. This dessert is a cherished family favorite that always feels like a warm hug. Just add your favorite vegan ice cream to a warm piece of this crisp.

———————————————

Preheat the oven to 350°F (180°C).

Make the filling: Place the pears, lemon juice, coconut sugar, cinnamon, cornstarch, and ¼ cup (60 mL) water in a large mixing bowl. Gently mix until the pears are well coated. Transfer the pear filling to a 9-inch pie dish or baking dish. Clean the mixing bowl, making sure it is completely dry.

Make the topping: In the same bowl, stir together the oats, almond flour, all-purpose flour, coconut sugar, walnuts, cinnamon, and coconut oil. Sprinkle the topping over the pear filling in an even layer.

Bake for 40 to 50 minutes, uncovered, until the filling is bubbling and the topping is golden brown.

Remove from the oven and let rest for 20 minutes before serving.

BLUEBERRY AND POPPY SEED MUFFINS WITH LEMON ICING DRIZZLE

MAKES 12 • PREP TIME: 15 MINUTES • COOK TIME: 35 MINUTES

1 tablespoon (15 mL) melted coconut oil, plus more for greasing the tin

1 cup (250 mL) unsweetened oat milk

⅔ cup (160 mL) maple syrup

¼ cup (60 mL) vegetable oil

1 tablespoon (15 mL) freshly squeezed lemon juice

1 tablespoon (15 mL) vanilla extract

1 teaspoon (5 mL) apple cider vinegar

2 cups (500 mL) all-purpose flour

3 tablespoons (45 mL) poppy seeds

2½ teaspoons (12.5 mL) baking powder

½ teaspoon (2.5 mL) baking soda

½ teaspoon (2.5 mL) kosher salt

1 cup (250 mL) fresh or frozen blueberries

3 tablespoons (45 mL) grated lemon zest, divided

FOR THE LEMON ICING DRIZZLE

½ cup (125 mL) confectioners' sugar

¼ cup (60 mL) freshly squeezed lemon juice

CHLOÉ WRITES: I'm sure everyone experiences those midday slumps where you're desperately in need of a pick-me-up. I know I certainly do, and my ultimate savior comes in the form of these muffins. These treats have become my go-to remedy whenever I feel my energy dwindling, and they never fail to bring me back to life, making my day a whole lot sweeter. I typically make them on Sunday, so I can grab one here and there throughout the week.

Preheat the oven to 350°F (180°C). Grease a 12-cup muffin tin with coconut oil.

In a large bowl, combine the coconut oil, oat milk, maple syrup, vegetable oil, lemon juice, vanilla, and vinegar. In another large bowl, whisk together the flour, poppy seeds, baking powder, baking soda, and salt.

Pour the wet ingredients into the dry ingredients and whisk together until smooth. Using a rubber spatula, fold in the blueberries.

Divide the batter evenly among the muffin cups and sprinkle with 2 tablespoons (30 mL) lemon zest. Bake for 30 to 35 minutes, or until a toothpick inserted into the middle of a muffin comes out clean. Remove from the oven and let cool for 30 minutes.

Make the lemon icing drizzle: In a small bowl, mix together the confectioners' sugar and lemon juice. Once the muffins are cool, drizzle with the icing and sprinkle with the remaining lemon zest.

SOLO SUPPERS

TRUDY WRITES: Eating alone can still be a time to enjoy a delicious meal. When Chloé or I eat alone, we have the same goal: to create a nutritious meal and a beautiful table. We will light a candle and use one of my handmade dishes and our favorite napkin to finish off the setting. Sometimes a book will come out or our computer will sit in front of us while we eat, but we like to think of this as a time to savor. We also look at it as an opportunity to be fully engaged in the flavors, textures, and aromas of the dishes we create without any distractions.

When Chloé first moved to New York and knew only a few people in the city, she often cooked alone at home (not a very New York thing to do, as so many people just order takeout). She was never lonely in these moments because she was fully invested in the meal she had just created and relished the opportunity it gave her to choose what she wanted to cook and the ambience she wanted to create in peaceful solitude.

So whether it's a simple meal or a feast you are looking to make, dining alone can be a wonderful occasion for self-care and self-indulgence.

TRAVEL MARKET SANDWICH

SERVES 1 • PREP TIME: 10 MINUTES

½ fresh baguette, 6 to 8 inches long

½ tablespoon (7.5 mL) extra-virgin olive oil

1 peach, sliced into thin wedges

1 heirloom tomato, sliced

1 scallion, sliced

2 teaspoons (10 mL) balsamic glaze or reduction

3 fresh basil leaves, roughly chopped

flaky sea salt and freshly ground black pepper

CHLOÉ WRITES: As a traveler who understands the need for simple, fresh food while on the go, I created this recipe for those moments when you find yourself with no kitchen. With readily accessible ingredients from around the world, the Travel Market Sandwich is the easiest and freshest thing to whip up, allowing you to have a homemade treat without the hassle of dining out for every meal.

Set the grill, if using, to 300°F (150°C).

Cut the baguette in half lengthwise and brush the cut sides with the olive oil. Toast the baguette halves in a toaster oven or on a hot grill if you have one available until the cut sides are golden brown, about 7 minutes.

Layer the peach wedges, tomato slices, and scallion on the bottom half of the toasted baguette. Drizzle with the balsamic glaze, then top with the basil and season with salt and pepper to taste. Cover with the top half of the baguette and enjoy.

VELVETY BROCCOLI SOUP

SERVES 6 • PREP TIME: 15 MINUTES • COOK TIME: 25 MINUTES

¼ cup (60 mL) extra-virgin olive oil,
  plus more for drizzle

1 large white onion, roughly chopped

2 medium white potatoes, peeled and cubed

4 garlic cloves, minced

2 teaspoons (10 mL) dried oregano

2 teaspoons (10 mL) dried thyme

½ teaspoon (2.5 mL) chili flakes

1 teaspoon (5 mL) sea salt

1 teaspoon (5 mL) freshly ground black pepper

8 cups (1.89 L) broccoli florets (2 large heads)

4 cups (1 L) vegetable broth

1 cup (250 mL) unsweetened oat milk

⅓ cup (80 mL) sliced almonds, for garnish

Warm up with this delicious and comforting broccoli soup recipe that is perfect for cozy evenings. With just a handful of simple ingredients and minimal effort, you can create a creamy, nutritious bowl of goodness that will leave you feeling satisfied and content. Get ready to enjoy a heartwarming soup that even broccoli skeptics will adore.

To a large pot over medium heat, add the olive oil, onion, and potatoes. When the onion and potatoes start to sizzle, add the garlic, oregano, thyme, chili flakes, salt, and pepper. Stir until the potatoes are coated with the spices. Add the broccoli florets and mix to incorporate. Add the vegetable broth and oat milk, stir, and bring to a boil. Once the mixture is boiling, reduce the heat to low and simmer until the potatoes and broccoli have softened, about 25 minutes.

Using an immersion blender, purée the soup in the pot, or transfer the soup in batches to a heat-resistant blender and purée until it reaches a creamy consistency, being careful not to splatter the soup.

Serve in individual bowls and garnish with the almonds and a drizzle of olive oil.

STORAGE: *This is great for leftovers! Store leftovers in an airtight container in the fridge for up to 3 to 5 days*

MEDITERRANEAN-STYLE CRISPY CHICKPEA LETTUCE WRAPS

MAKES 3 LETTUCE WRAPS; SERVES 1
PREP TIME: 10 MINUTES · COOK TIME: 20 MINUTES

⅓ cup (80 mL) canned chickpeas, drained and rinsed

⅓ cup (80 mL) sliced white onion

2 tablespoons (30 mL) extra-virgin olive oil, divided

½ teaspoon (2.5 mL) cayenne pepper

⅓ cup (80 mL) white quinoa

1 teaspoon (5 mL) ground cumin

1 teaspoon (5 mL) ground sumac

1 small Persian cucumber, diced

1 small Roma tomato, diced

1 teaspoon (5 mL) dried thyme

1 teaspoon (5 mL) lemon pepper

kosher salt and freshly ground black pepper

⅓ cup (80 mL) unsweetened plain vegan yogurt, such as almond or cashew

2 teaspoons (10 mL) thinly sliced fresh chives

1 tablespoon (15 mL) freshly squeezed lemon juice

2 teaspoons (10 mL) freshly grated lemon zest

3 large romaine lettuce leaves

¼ cup (60 mL) sliced scallions, for garnish

1 teaspoon (5 mL) sea salt

This easy recipe incorporates the richness of Mediterranean ingredients with the crunch of crispy chickpeas nestled in fresh lettuce wraps. The combination of aromatic herbs, tangy cucumber, juicy tomato, and zesty lemon dressing creates a symphony of flavors that will leave you craving more. Perfect for a quick lunch, these wraps are not only delicious but packed with nutrients, making them a guilt-free, wholesome choice to satisfy your midday cravings.

Preheat the oven to 400°F (200°C) (see Note).

Place the chickpeas, onion, 1 tablespoon (15 mL) olive oil, and the cayenne pepper into a large bowl. Mix well to coat the chickpeas and onion evenly.

Place the chickpea mixture on a baking sheet and bake for about 15 minutes, until the chickpeas and onion are crispy and golden brown. Remove from the oven and set aside.

To a medium pot, add the quinoa, ¾ cup (180 mL) water, the cumin, and sumac. Bring to a boil over medium heat and cover. Reduce the heat to medium-low and simmer for 15 minutes. Remove the pot from the heat and let sit, covered, for 5 minutes.

In a large bowl, combine the cucumber, tomato, thyme, lemon pepper, and the remaining 1 tablespoon (15 mL) olive oil. Add the cooked quinoa to the bowl, season with salt and black pepper to taste, and mix well. ➤➤

◄◄ In a small bowl, whisk together the yogurt, chives, lemon juice, and lemon zest.

On each lettuce leaf, spread 1 tablespoon (15 mL) of the yogurt mixture followed by one-third of the chickpea mixture. Top with the scallions and sea salt.

NOTE: *You can also use an air fryer set to 400°F (200°C) to crisp the chickpea mixture.*

GRILLED BAGUETTE WITH CARAMELIZED MUSHROOMS, BALSAMIC TAHINI BUTTER, AND SHAVED PARMESAN

MAKES 2 TOASTS   •   PREP TIME: 15 MINUTES   •   COOK TIME: 15 MINUTES

½ cup (125 mL) canned chickpeas, drained and rinsed

2 tablespoons (30 mL) extra-virgin olive oil, divided

½ teaspoon (2.5 mL) cayenne pepper

1 cup (250 mL) sliced red onion
(half of a medium onion)

2 garlic cloves, minced

3 cups (750 mL) sliced mushrooms,
such as a combination of cremini,
shiitake, maitake, chanterelles, and portobello

1 tablespoon (15 mL) vegan butter

1 teaspoon (5 mL) Italian seasoning

1 teaspoon (5 mL) ground cumin

½ teaspoon (2.5 mL) kosher salt

½ teaspoon (2.5 mL) freshly ground black pepper

½ fresh baguette, 6 to 8 inches long,
sliced in half horizontally

1 tablespoon (15 mL) store-bought or homemade
chimichurri (see page 55)

2 tablespoons (30 mL) shaved vegan parmesan,
for topping

1 tablespoon (15 mL) roughly chopped fresh dill,
for topping

FOR THE BALSAMIC TAHINI BUTTER

1 tablespoon (15 mL) tahini

1 tablespoon (15 mL) balsamic glaze or reduction

2 teaspoons (10 mL) apple cider vinegar

This recipe is designed with the solo diner in mind, making it effortless to prepare a delicious meal for one. With only a few ingredients and minimal cooking equipment, you can enjoy this dish without worrying about creating leftovers or spending too much time in the kitchen.

Preheat the oven to 375°F (190°C).

Place the chickpeas on a baking sheet, coat with ½ tablespoon (7.5 mL) olive oil, and sprinkle with the cayenne pepper. Bake for about 15 minutes, until the chickpeas become golden and crispy. Remove from the oven and set aside.

Into a medium pan over medium-low heat, drizzle the remaining 1½ tablespoons (22.5 mL) olive oil. When it starts to shimmer, add the onion and garlic and cook, stirring, until the onion has softened, 3 to 4 minutes. Raise the heat to medium and add the mushrooms, vegan butter, Italian seasoning, cumin, salt, and black pepper. Cook, stirring, until the mushrooms have caramelized, about 10 to 15 minutes. Remove from the heat and transfer to a bowl.

Put the two baguette halves into the same pan, cut side down, and crisp for about 1 minute.

Make the tahini butter: In a small bowl, whisk together the tahini, balsamic glaze, vinegar, and 2 teaspoons (10 mL) water to create a smooth, buttery texture.

Smear the tahini butter onto the baguette halves and top with the caramelized onion and mushroom mixture, crispy chickpeas, chimichurri, parmesan, and dill.

SQUASH AND VEGAN PUTTANESCA PIZZA

MAKES 1 PIZZA • COOK TIME: 30 MINUTES
PREP TIME: 30 MINUTES, PLUS 6 HOURS TO THAW THE PIZZA DOUGH

one 19-ounce (500 g) package store-bought frozen pizza dough

2 tablespoons (30 mL) extra-virgin olive oil, divided

1 medium delicata squash

½ cup (125 mL) sliced red onion

3 garlic cloves, minced

1 teaspoon (5 mL) kosher salt

1 teaspoon (5 mL) freshly ground black pepper

3 cups (750 mL) kale, stems removed and leaves roughly chopped

½ cup (125 mL) store-bought vegan puttanesca sauce

1 large heirloom tomato, cut into 6 slices

1 cup (250 mL) canned fire-roasted bell peppers, drained and sliced

1 cup (250 mL) shredded vegan mozzarella

½ cup (125 mL) sun-dried tomatoes in oil, sliced

1 teaspoon (5 mL) chili oil, for topping

CHLOÉ WRITES: Picture this: It's a chilly autumn evening, and the aroma of freshly baked pizza fills the air. The roasted squash adds a touch of comforting sweetness that perfectly balances the savory elements. I remember the first time I made this recipe; it instantly became a fall and winter favorite in my household. With every bite, it felt like a warm hug from the inside, making it a delicious meal to satisfy any pizza lover during the colder months.

Thaw the pizza dough in the fridge for 6 hours before making the pizza. Preheat the oven to 425°F (220°C).

Once the dough has thawed, oil a baking sheet with 1 tablespoon (15 mL) olive oil and stretch the dough to cover the entire surface of the baking sheet.

With a sharp knife, remove the stem and bottom of the squash. Using a spoon, scoop out the seeds and strings from inside the squash. Slice into 10 rings.

Add the remaining 1 tablespoon (15 mL) olive oil to a large skillet over medium-low heat. When it starts to shimmer, add the onion and cook, stirring, until caramelized, about 10 minutes. Add the squash, garlic, salt, and pepper and cook, stirring, until the squash softens slightly, about 5 minutes. Transfer the contents of the skillet to a large bowl. To the same skillet over medium heat, add the kale and cook, stirring, until bright green and slightly wilted, about 2 minutes. Set aside.

Spread the puttanesca sauce over the prepared dough, leaving a ½-inch border. Evenly layer the heirloom tomato, bell peppers, and squash on the dough and top with the mozzarella. ➵

◂◂ Bake for 16 to 20 minutes, until the crust turns golden brown. Remove from the oven, add the kale and sun-dried tomatoes, and top with the chili oil.

STORAGE: *Wrap any leftover pizza in plastic wrap and store in the fridge for up to 3 days. It makes a great lunch or snack.*

MARINATED TEMPEH RICE BOWL WITH COCONUT-LIME RICE, STEAMED VEGETABLES, AND ALMOND SAUCE

SERVES 2 TO 4 · PREP TIME: 30 MINUTES · COOK TIME: 10 MINUTES

8 ounces (240 g) tempeh, cut into thin slices

2 tablespoons (30 mL) tamari

2 tablespoons (30 mL) sesame oil

2 tablespoons (30 mL) freshly squeezed lime juice, divided

1 tablespoon (15 mL) maple syrup

1 garlic clove, finely grated

½ teaspoon (2.5 mL) finely grated fresh ginger

1 cup (250 mL) basmati rice

1 teaspoon (5 mL) coconut oil

kosher salt

1 cup (250 mL) unsweetened coconut milk

4 broccolini stalks, cut lengthwise

1 large carrot, sliced lengthwise

1 small zucchini, sliced lengthwise

1 teaspoon (5 mL) grapeseed oil
  or other neutral-flavored oil

lime wedges, for serving

1 scallion, thinly sliced, for garnish

FOR THE ALMOND SAUCE

⅓ cup (80 mL) unsweetened creamy almond butter

1 tablespoon (15 mL) sesame oil

½ tablespoon (7.5 mL) tamari

2 tablespoons (30 mL) freshly squeezed lime juice

2 teaspoons (10 mL) chopped fresh ginger

1 garlic clove

kosher salt

TRUDY SAYS: I can't get enough of this marinated tempeh rice bowl. It's the best meal, no matter if it's freezing cold or scorching hot outside. During winter, the spices in the tempeh marinade warm me up and make me feel all cozy inside. Then comes summer, and I start craving the colorful veggies and tangy coconut-lime rice—it's like a burst of freshness in every bite. No matter the time of year, the creamy almond sauce drizzled over the bowl takes this dish to a whole new level.

In a medium bowl, combine the tempeh, tamari, sesame oil, 1 tablespoon (15 mL) lime juice, the maple syrup, garlic, and ginger and gently toss to combine. Let the tempeh marinate for at least 30 minutes.

Meanwhile, rinse the rice under cold water until the water runs clear. Melt the coconut oil in a small heavy-bottomed saucepan with a lid over medium heat. Add the rice and a pinch of salt and stir well to coat the rice with the oil. Add the coconut milk and ½ cup (125 mL) water and stir continuously until the liquid comes to a boil. Once boiling, reduce the heat to low, cover the pot, and allow to simmer until all the liquid has been absorbed, 8 to 10 minutes. Remove from the heat and place a piece of paper towel between the pot and the lid to absorb the steam and create fluffy rice. Stir the remaining 1 tablespoon (15 mL) lime juice into the rice before serving.

Make the sauce: To a high-speed blender, add the almond butter, ¼ cup (60 mL) water, the sesame oil, tamari, lime juice, ginger, garlic, and a pinch of salt and blend until very smooth. ➤

◂◂ Place the broccolini, carrot, and zucchini into a steamer basket placed over a pot of simmering water and steam until tender— about 10 minutes for the carrot and 5 to 8 minutes for the broccolini and zucchini.

While the vegetables are steaming, pour the grapeseed oil into a cast-iron skillet or a heavy-bottomed pan, add the tempeh and marinade, and cook for about 2 minutes on each side, or until the tempeh has absorbed the marinade and is sticky and caramelized.

Serve the veggies and tempeh over the rice, drizzled generously with the almond sauce and a squeeze of lime juice, and topped with the sliced scallions.

STORAGE: *Keep any leftovers in glass containers in the fridge for up to 4 days.*

TARTINES WITH PEAS, RICOTTA, AND BEET HUMMUS

SERVES 1 OR 2 • PREP TIME: 10 MINUTES • COOK TIME: 5 MINUTES

1 cup (250 mL) fresh peas

2 slices multigrain bread

⅓ cup (80 mL) panko bread crumbs

½ cup (125 mL) vegan ricotta

¼ cup (60 mL) vegan pesto,
   store-bought or homemade (see page 36)

⅓ cup (80 mL) beet hummus (see page 29)

¼ cup (60 mL) sliced shallot

2 tablespoons (30 mL) sliced scallion

¼ cup (60 mL) pea sprouts

1 teaspoon (5 mL) chili oil

lemon wedges

TRUDY WRITES: This is an easy weeknight solo supper. Chloé came up with this recipe, and it is a favorite for me. I often work late in the studio, and when I get home, I want a quick meal that is light and nutritious. This fits those criteria perfectly, with a delicious combination of flavors.

Bring a small pot of water to a boil over high heat. Add the peas and cook for 5 minutes. Drain and set aside.

While the peas are cooking, toast the bread.

In a large bowl, place the cooked peas, panko, and ricotta and mix until combined. Add the pesto and mix to coat evenly.

Spread the hummus on both slices of bread, followed by the pea and ricotta mixture. Top with the shallot, scallion, pea sprouts, chili oil, and a squeeze of lemon juice.

BLOOD ORANGE ENDIVE SALAD WITH CRUNCHY RADISHES

SERVES 1 TO 2 · PREP TIME: 10 MINUTES

10 endive leaves

4 radishes, cut into halves

⅓ cup (80 mL) sliced shallot

1 blood orange, peeled and cut into 8 slices,
    plus 1 teaspoon grated zest for topping

¼ cup (60 mL) chopped unsalted walnuts, for topping

kosher salt and freshly ground black pepper

FOR THE DRESSING

2 tablespoons (30 mL) olive oil

1 tablespoon (15 mL) red wine vinegar

1 tablespoon (15 mL) whole grain mustard

1 teaspoon (5 mL) maple syrup

This delicious salad captures the essence of sun-soaked days, combining the juicy sweetness of blood oranges with the crisp bitterness of endive. Topped with a mustard dressing and accompanied by crunchy radishes, this salad is a burst of sunshine on your plate.

Arrange the endive leaves, radishes, shallot, and orange slices on a large plate.

Make the dressing: In a small bowl, whisk together the olive oil, vinegar, mustard, and maple syrup until emulsified.

Drizzle the dressing over the salad, sprinkle with the blood orange zest, and top with the walnuts. Season to taste with salt and pepper.

TRADITIONAL GREEK SALAD

SERVES 1 TO 2 • PREP TIME: 10 MINUTES

1 large tomato, cut into wedges

½ red bell pepper, seeded and cut into large pieces

½ green bell pepper, seeded and cut into large pieces

2 Persian cucumbers, cut into slices or half moons

½ white onion, sliced

¼ cup (60 mL) pitted kalamata olives

juice of 1 lemon

2 teaspoons (10 mL) extra-virgin olive oil

kosher salt and freshly ground black pepper

1 thick slice vegan feta,
    cut in half on the diagonal

1 teaspoon (5 mL) dried oregano

Step into the flavors of Greece with this classic salad recipe. As the warm summer sun bathes the picturesque landscapes of this Mediterranean gem, locals and tourists alike seek solace in the iconic flavors. Imagine yourself seated at a seaside taverna, savoring the vibrant combination of crisp cucumbers, juicy tomatoes, tangy vegan feta cheese, briny olives, and aromatic herbs, all drizzled with a lemony olive oil dressing.

Place the tomato, red and green bell peppers, cucumbers, onion, and olives into a large serving bowl. Drizzle with the lemon juice and olive oil and season to taste with salt and pepper. Top with the feta and oregano.

CORN FRITTERS WITH
AVOCADO SMASH AND ARUGULA SALAD

MAKES 8 · PREP TIME: 20 MINUTES · COOK TIME: 20 MINUTES

½ cup (125 mL) all-purpose flour

¼ cup (60 mL) fine cornmeal

1 tablespoon (15 mL) nutritional yeast

½ teaspoon (2.5 mL) baking powder

½ teaspoon (2.5 mL) kosher salt

½ teaspoon (2.5 mL) smoked paprika

freshly ground black pepper

½ cup (125 mL) unsweetened plant milk,
such as almond or soy

1 cup (250 mL) frozen or fresh corn kernels

¼ cup (60 mL) frozen green peas

¼ cup (60 ml) finely diced red onion

1 scallion, finely chopped

½ cup (125 mL) minced mixed fresh herbs,
such as basil, cilantro, Italian parsley, or mint

3 tablespoons (45 mL) extra-virgin olive oil
or neutral-flavored oil

1 cup (250 mL) arugula leaves, washed and dried

handful of cherry tomatoes, halved

FOR THE AVOCADO SMASH

2 avocados

3 tablespoons (45 mL) freshly squeezed lemon juice

½ teaspoon (2.5 mL) kosher salt

freshly ground black pepper

For a savory solo supper, these corn fritters hit the spot. We like to keep some extras on hand for quick, satisfying lunches during the week—simply freeze them and grab a couple when needed. To add a touch of freshness, we love pairing them with avocado smash.

In a medium bowl, whisk together the flour, cornmeal, nutritional yeast, baking powder, salt, paprika, and a few grinds of pepper. Add the plant milk and whisk to form a smooth batter. Fold in the corn, peas, onion, scallion, and herbs until everything is well coated in batter.

Make the avocado smash: Cut the avocados in half, remove the pit, and scoop the avocado flesh into a medium bowl. Drizzle with the lemon juice and smash with a fork until the desired consistency is reached. Season with the salt and a few grinds of pepper and set aside while you make the fritters.

In a large heavy-bottomed pan, heat the oil over medium heat until it starts to shimmer, about 2 minutes. Using a ¼-cup (60-mL) measure, carefully spoon the batter into the hot oil. Cook until a nice golden color, about 3 minutes on each side.

Serve the fritters hot, topped with the avocado smash, arugula, and cherry tomatoes.

STORAGE: *Any leftover fritters can be wrapped in plastic and stored in the freezer for a couple of months for a quick, easy meal anytime. Reheat them for 1 minute in the microwave before serving. The leftover avocado smash can be stored in a glass container in the fridge for a couple of days.*

SWEET POTATO AND ENDIVE SALAD

SERVES 1 TO 2 · PREP TIME: 10 MINUTES · COOK TIME: 20 MINUTES

1 medium sweet potato,
    skin on, washed, cut into 8 wedges

2 teaspoons (10 mL) extra-virgin olive oil

kosher salt and freshly ground black pepper

½ cup (125 mL) spreadable vegan cheese

2 endive heads, leaves separated

½ cup (125 mL) chopped radicchio

⅓ cup (80 mL) sliced shallot

8 teaspoons (40 mL) store-bought or homemade
    chimichurri (see page 55)

1 fresh red chile pepper, sliced into discs

Sweet potatoes hold a special place among our favorite vegetables. They find their way into countless recipes, and even a simple stuffed sweet potato makes for a satisfying, easy meal. We make it a point to keep these versatile gems readily available in our fridge. Whether roasted, fried, or baked, their natural sweetness adds great flavor to a dish.

Preheat the oven to 400°F (200°C).

Place the sweet potato on a baking pan, coat with the olive oil, and season with salt and pepper. Bake for 20 minutes, until cooked through and golden brown.

Spread 1 tablespoon (15 mL) of the vegan cheese on each endive leaf. Add 1 tablespoon (15 mL) of the chopped radicchio and top with 1 sweet potato wedge, ½ tablespoon (7.5 mL) of the shallot, 1 teaspoon (5 mL) of the chimichurri, and 1 slice of fresh red chile pepper.

STRAWBERRY OAT BARS

MAKES 8 • PREP TIME: 10 MINUTES • COOK TIME: 30 MINUTES

2 cups (500 mL) oat flour

1 cup (250 mL) rolled oats

2 tablespoons (30 mL) chia seeds

1 cup (250 mL) unsweetened almond milk

1 cup (250 mL) unsweetened plain vegan
    coconut yogurt

1 flax egg: 1 tablespoon (15 mL) flaxseed meal
    stirred into 2 tablespoons (30 mL) warm water

⅓ cup (80 mL) maple syrup

2 tablespoons (30 mL) unsweetened creamy
    almond butter

1 teaspoon (5 mL) vanilla extract

1 cup (250 mL) fresh strawberries, hulled and diced

These are perfect to satisfy your midday cravings or have as a dessert treat. Packed with wholesome ingredients such as rolled oats, fresh strawberries, and a hint of maple syrup, these bars have a great balance of flavors and textures. They are sure to become your new favorite treat.

Preheat the oven to 375°F (190°C) and line an 8-inch square cake pan with parchment paper, leaving a lip of parchment.

In a large bowl, whisk together the oat flour, oats, and chia seeds. In a separate large bowl, combine the almond milk, yogurt, flax egg, maple syrup, almond butter, and vanilla.

Pour the wet ingredients into the dry ingredients and mix until well combined. Add the strawberries.

Pour the batter into the prepared cake pan and bake for about 30 minutes, or until golden brown. Remove from the oven and let cool in the pan for 20 minutes. Once cool, cut into 8 bars.

STORAGE: *The bars can be stored in the fridge for up to 5 days or in the freezer for up to 4 weeks.*

NO-BAKE CHOCOLATE COCONUT BARS

MAKES 8 · PREP TIME: 15 MINUTES, PLUS 2 HOURS TO REFRIGERATE

½ cup (125 mL) rolled oats

¾ cup (180 mL) unsalted roasted almonds

¾ cup (180 mL) unsweetened shredded coconut

4 dates, soaked in hot water for 5 minutes

3 tablespoons (45 mL) cacao powder

3 tablespoons (45 mL) melted coconut oil, divided

2 tablespoons (30 mL) hemp seeds

1 tablespoon (15 mL) maple syrup

½ teaspoon (2.5 mL) vanilla extract

2.8 ounces (80 g) vegan chocolate, melted

flaky sea salt

CHLOÉ SAYS: We like to make these bars during the week, and the best part is that they're easy to keep in the fridge. Trudy takes one to her pottery studio, and I pack a couple whenever I'm on the go. We both always find ourselves craving a snack around 3:00 p.m. that not only satisfies our sweet tooth but also provides a burst of energy. These no-bake chocolate coconut bars come to the rescue and are the perfect blend of wholesome ingredients and chocolate goodness.

Line an 8-inch square cake pan with parchment paper.

To a food processor, add the oats, almonds, shredded coconut, dates, cacao powder, 2 tablespoons (30 mL) melted coconut oil, hemp seeds, maple syrup, and vanilla. Process until you have a dough that sticks together in a ball. Press the dough into the bottom of the prepared pan until the top is smooth and even.

Stir the remaining 1 tablespoon (15 mL) coconut oil into the melted chocolate and spread evenly over the dough.

Place in the fridge, uncovered, to chill for at least 2 hours. Remove from the pan, sprinkle with sea salt, and slice into 8 bars.

STORAGE: *These bars can be stored in the fridge for up to 5 days or in the freezer for up to 3 months.*

CHLOÉ WRITES: We love weekend mornings, relishing the opportunity to sleep in and go at a slower pace. A wonderful ritual for me involves taking my dog for a leisurely walk and stopping to pick up a cup of coffee on my way home. My mom's is sitting on her couch with the sun streaming in and reading from one of her large array of coffee table books.

A special moment when I was growing up was making Saturday-morning pancakes. In my younger years, my mom would involve me in the process; I would mix the ingredients in the bowl, and then she would shape the pancakes into fun animal or heart forms. As I grew older and ventured out on my own, that cherished tradition has endured. Even though we now live miles apart, both of us continue to make pancakes on the weekends.

For brunch, our go-to recipes are Veggie Tofu Scramble (page 259) and Pancakes with Blueberry Coulis (page 236), which are loved by everyone. These are perfect not only for a late brunch gathering but also for a satisfying solo indulgence. And let's not forget the irresistible smell of freshly baked Dark Chocolate Chip Coconut Banana Bread (page 256), enjoyed warm and straight from the oven!

MORNING MUESLI COOKIES

MAKES 10 · PREP TIME: 5 MINUTES · COOK TIME: 15 MINUTES

1½ cups (375 mL) muesli (see Note)

½ cup (125 mL) all-purpose flour

½ cup (125 mL) unsweetened plain vegan yogurt, such as cashew or almond

½ cup (125 mL) melted coconut oil

6 tablespoons (90 mL) maple syrup

¼ cup (60 mL) unsweetened smooth almond butter

2 tablespoons (30 mL) apple cider vinegar

CHLOÉ WRITES: This recipe was born of a desire for a quick, easy homemade treat that wouldn't compromise on taste or nutrition. It all started one busy afternoon when I found myself craving something sweet but lacking the time and energy to embark on a full-fledged baking adventure. Determined to create a treat that would satisfy my sweet tooth, I rummaged through my pantry and stumbled upon a jar of muesli. Inspired by its wholesome ingredients, I decided to transform it into a cookie. After a few rounds of experimentation, the recipe emerged as the perfect blend of simplicity, flavor, and satisfaction.

Preheat the oven to 350°F (180°C) and line a large baking pan with parchment paper.

In a large bowl, mix the muesli, flour, yogurt, coconut oil, maple syrup, almond butter, and vinegar until fully combined.

Scoop 2 tablespoons (30 mL) of the dough onto the prepared pan and press down lightly with the bottom of a glass. Repeat with the rest of the dough, spacing 1 inch apart (they won't spread). Bake for about 15 minutes, until golden brown. Remove from the oven and cool on a wire rack for 20 minutes before eating.

NOTE: *If you don't have muesli on hand, you can use 1 cup (250 mL) rolled oats, ½ cup (125 mL) dried fruit, and ¼ cup (60 mL) chopped nuts and seeds.*

STORAGE: *The cookies can be stored in an airtight container for up to 5 days.*

PANCAKES WITH BLUEBERRY COULIS

MAKES 8 · PREP TIME: 20 MINUTES · COOK TIME: 15 MINUTES

FOR THE PANCAKES

1⅓ cups (330 mL) all-purpose flour

1 teaspoon (5 mL) baking soda

1 teaspoon (5 mL) baking powder

1⅓ cups (330 mL) plant milk, such as almond or soy

1 tablespoon (15 mL) melted coconut oil

1 tablespoon (15 mL) maple syrup

1 flax egg: 1 tablespoon (15 mL) flaxseed meal
stirred into 2 tablespoons (30 mL) warm water

2 tablespoons (30 mL) extra-virgin olive oil, divided

FOR THE COULIS

2 cups (500 mL) fresh or frozen blueberries

1 tablespoon (15 mL) chia seeds

1 tablespoon (15 mL) freshly squeezed lemon juice

1 teaspoon (5 mL) maple syrup

CHLOÉ WRITES: This vegan pancake recipe with blueberry coulis has been a staple in our house since I was a child, and it's a Saturday tradition that I absolutely adore. We hope this easy, fluffy, healthy breakfast will become a weekend favorite in your home as well.

Make the pancakes: In a large bowl, mix together the flour, baking soda, and baking powder.

In a separate medium bowl, combine the milk, coconut oil, maple syrup, and flax egg and mix well. Slowly pour the wet ingredients into the dry ingredients, mixing continuously until a beautiful pancake batter has formed, about 30 seconds.

Heat a medium frying pan over medium heat and coat the pan with 1 teaspoon (5 mL) olive oil. When it starts to shimmer, pour ⅓ cup (80 mL) of batter into the pan and cook for 1 to 2 minutes on each side until a nice golden-brown color. Repeat, adding oil as necessary, until all the batter has been used.

Make the coulis: Place 2 tablespoons (30 mL) water and the blueberries into a small pot and bring to a simmer. Once the blueberries start oozing their beautiful dark blue color, add the chia seeds, lemon juice, and maple syrup. Stir gently until the coulis thickens, about 3 minutes. Pour into a sauce boat and serve alongside the pancakes.

RASPBERRY BUTTER VANILLA LOAF

MAKES ONE 9-INCH LOAF • PREP TIME: 10 MINUTES • COOK TIME: 45 MINUTES

1 tablespoon (15 mL) avocado oil,
   plus more for greasing the pan

2 cups (500 mL) all-purpose flour

1 cup (250 mL) packed light brown sugar

1 teaspoon (5 mL) baking powder

1 teaspoon (5 mL) baking soda

1 cup (250 mL) unsweetened oat milk

⅓ cup (80 mL) melted vegan butter,
   plus 2 tablespoons (30 mL) for topping

1 tablespoon (15 mL) distilled white vinegar

2 teaspoons (10 mL) vanilla extract

½ cup (125 mL) raspberry jam

1 pint (500 g) fresh raspberries, halved

Imagine waking up on a lazy weekend morning, craving a delicious, sweet treat that doubles as a breakfast delight. That's exactly what led us on a quest to create the ultimate easy cake—one that would satisfy both dessert desires and early-morning cravings. Little did we know that our testing would lead us to this raspberry butter vanilla loaf, a heavenly confection that bridges the gap between a delectable dessert and a sweet breakfast option.

Preheat the oven to 350°F (180°C) and grease a 9-by-5-inch loaf pan.

Sift the flour into a large bowl. Add the brown sugar, baking powder, and baking soda and lightly mix. To the same bowl, add 1 tablespoon (15 mL) avocado oil, the oat milk, ⅓ cup (80 mL) vegan butter, 1 tablespoon (15 mL) water, the vinegar, and vanilla and whisk until evenly mixed and there are no big lumps. Don't overmix; small lumps are fine.

Pour the batter into the prepared loaf pan and bake for about 45 minutes, or until a toothpick inserted into the middle comes out clean. If needed, bake for another 5 minutes. Remove from the oven and let cool thoroughly.

In a medium bowl, whisk together the raspberry jam and 2 tablespoons (30 mL) vegan butter. Spread the raspberry butter evenly over the cooled cake and arrange the halved raspberries on top.

BLUEBERRY COCONUT OVERNIGHT OATS WITH SUMMER FRUITS

SERVES 2 • PREP TIME: 10 MINUTES, PLUS OVERNIGHT TO SOAK

1 cup (250 mL) rolled oats

1 cup (250 mL) unsweetened almond milk

1 cup (250 mL) unsweetened plain vegan
    coconut yogurt, divided

2 tablespoons (30 mL) chia seeds

2 tablespoons (30 mL) maple syrup

¼ cup (60 mL) fresh blueberries,
    plus more for topping

1 cup (250 mL) fresh mixed berries,
    such as raspberries, currants, and strawberries,
    for topping

1 plum, cut into wedges, for topping

2 tablespoons (30 mL) unsweetened shredded
    coconut, for topping

TRUDY SAYS: A little ritual that has been a game changer for me is preparing this recipe the night before and having it ready to eat for breakfast the next day. It is a delicious start to the day, with protein, fruit, and fiber that is good for you.

Combine the oats, almond milk, ½ cup (125 mL) coconut yogurt, the chia seeds, and maple syrup in a medium bowl and mix well. Add ¼ cup (60 mL) blueberries, mix to combine, cover, and refrigerate overnight.

Top with more blueberries, the mixed berries, plum wedges, the remaining ½ cup (125 mL) coconut yogurt, and the shredded coconut.

CHERRY AND RHUBARB RUSTIC TART

SERVES 6 · PREP TIME: 10 MINUTES · COOK TIME: 25 TO 30 MINUTES

one 14-ounce (397 g) vegan puff pastry sheet

1½ cups (375 mL) sliced fresh rhubarb

1 cup (250 mL) pitted cherries, halved

½ cup (125 mL) coconut sugar

⅓ cup (80 mL) almond flour

2 tablespoons (30 mL) cornstarch

2 tablespoons (30 mL) freshly squeezed lemon juice

2 teaspoons (10 mL) vanilla extract

1 tablespoon (15 mL) melted coconut oil

CHLOÉ SAYS: As I wandered through the local market in the Hudson Valley, surrounded by an abundance of fresh produce, I couldn't resist the vibrant seasonal offerings. Inspired by the luscious rhubarb and juicy cherries, I created a tart that perfectly captures the essence of summer's bounty.

Remove the pastry sheet from the freezer and thaw in the fridge 1 hour prior to baking.

Preheat the oven to 400°F (200°C). Line a baking sheet with parchment paper.

Place the rhubarb and cherries into a large bowl. Add the coconut sugar, almond flour, cornstarch, lemon juice, and vanilla and toss together.

On the prepared baking sheet, roll the pastry dough into a 10- to 12-inch circle. Pour the rhubarb and cherry mixture into the middle and fold the edges of the dough onto the filling, pleating and pressing together any cracks.

Brush the edges with the coconut oil and bake for 25 to 30 minutes, until the pastry is golden brown. Allow the tart to cool for 10 minutes before serving.

GRANOLA CRUNCH MEDLEY
WITH DRIED FRUITS

SERVES 12 • PREP TIME: 8 MINUTES • COOK TIME: 25 MINUTES

3 cups (750 mL) rolled oats

½ cup (125 mL) unsalted roasted almonds,
    roughly chopped

¼ cup (60 mL) raw cashews, roughly chopped

¼ cup (60 mL) raw sunflower seeds

¼ cup (60 mL) pumpkin seeds

¼ cup (60 mL) hemp hearts

¼ cup (60 mL) chia seeds

1 cup (250 mL) melted coconut oil

½ cup (125 mL) maple syrup

⅓ cup (80 mL) dried mulberries or cranberries

⅓ cup (80 mL) dark raisins

⅓ cup (80 mL) diced dried figs or prunes

CHLOÉ WRITES: I used to be often bloated, and it was the worst. I created this granola to alleviate bloating and kick-start the day with a satisfying, wholesome breakfast. Packed with fiber-rich ingredients and gut-friendly nutrients, this recipe soothes the digestive system while providing a delicious boost of energy.

Preheat the oven to 350°F (180°C) and line a baking sheet with parchment paper.

In a large bowl, mix together the oats, almonds, cashews, sunflower seeds, pumpkin seeds, hemp hearts, and chia seeds. Add the coconut oil and maple syrup and mix until well combined and the oats, seeds, and nuts are evenly coated.

Pour the mixture onto the prepared baking sheet and, using a large spatula, spread into an even layer. Bake for 20 to 25 minutes, until golden brown, stirring halfway through.

Remove from the oven and let cool for 30 minutes; this lets the granola crisp up even more. Add the mulberries, raisins, and figs or prunes and stir together.

STORAGE: *Keep the granola in a glass jar with a lid or an airtight container for up to 2 weeks.*

SPICED CARROT MUFFINS

MAKES 12　·　PREP TIME: 15 MINUTES　·　COOK TIME: 35 MINUTES

½ cup (125 mL) neutral-flavored oil, such as grapeseed or rice bran oil, plus more for greasing the tin

3 cups (750 mL) spelt flour

1½ cups (375 mL) packed coconut sugar

2½ teaspoons (12.5 mL) baking powder

½ teaspoon (2.5 mL) baking soda

2 teaspoons (10 mL) ground cinnamon

½ teaspoon (2.5 mL) ground ginger

¼ teaspoon (1.25 mL) ground cardamom

¼ teaspoon (1.25 mL) ground nutmeg

¾ cup (180 mL) chopped salted walnuts

1 tablespoon (15 mL) chia seeds

1 tablespoon (15 mL) flaxseed meal

2 cups (500 mL) peeled, grated carrots

1½ cups (375 mL) unsweetened plant milk, such as almond

1 tablespoon (15 mL) apple cider vinegar

1 teaspoon (5 mL) vanilla extract

FOR THE CRUMB TOPPING

⅓ cup (80 mL) spelt flour

¼ cup (60 mL) rolled oats

3 tablespoons (45 mL) cold vegan butter, cut into cubes

3 tablespoons (45 mL) coconut sugar

½ teaspoon (2.5 mL) ground cinnamon

These muffins hold a special place in our hearts and the hearts of all who gather around our brunch table. Each time we serve a batch of these, we are asked for the recipe. Whether for a planned celebration or a spontaneous weekend get-together, these muffins are a staple on our brunch menu. They are so much fun to make with friends and involve everyone working in the kitchen.

Preheat the oven to 350°F (180°C) and grease a 12-cup muffin tin with oil.

Into a medium bowl, sift together the flour, coconut sugar, baking powder, baking soda, cinnamon, ginger, cardamom, and nutmeg. Add the walnuts, chia seeds, and flaxseed meal and stir to combine.

In another medium bowl, whisk together the carrots, plant milk, ½ cup (125 mL) oil, the vinegar, and vanilla.

Add the wet ingredients to the dry ingredients and fold gently until just combined. Divide the batter evenly among the muffin cups.

Make the crumb topping: Combine the flour, oats, vegan butter, coconut sugar, and cinnamon in a medium bowl and crumble until there is no loose flour. Press a spoonful of the crumble onto the top of each muffin.

Bake for about 30 minutes. Insert a toothpick into a muffin; if it comes out clean, remove from the oven and let cool. If the toothpick is sticky, cook for another 5 minutes.

STORAGE: *Keep the muffins in an airtight container in the fridge for up to 5 days or in the freezer for up to 2 months.*

COCONUT QUINOA PORRIDGE WITH WARM STRAWBERRIES AND ALMOND BUTTER

SERVES 2 • PREP TIME: 10 MINUTES • COOK TIME: 15 MINUTES

¾ cup (180 mL) white quinoa

1 cup (250 mL) unsweetened coconut milk

3 tablespoons (45 mL) maple syrup, divided

1 teaspoon (5 mL) vanilla extract, divided

½ teaspoon (2.5 mL) ground cinnamon

1 pint strawberries, hulled and sliced

2 tablespoons (30 mL) almond butter, for topping

2 tablespoons (30 mL) raw slivered almonds,
    for topping

almond milk, for serving

This recipe reminds us of our time in Mallorca, wrapped in a cozy blanket while enjoying the mountain view and sound of birds. This velvety porridge feels like a warm hug. It's so important to embrace slow mornings, wherever you are.

Rinse the quinoa well to avoid a bitter taste. In a medium saucepan, bring the quinoa and 1½ cups (375 mL) water to a boil over high heat. Reduce the heat to low, cover the pan, and simmer until most of the liquid has been absorbed and the quinoa is tender, about 12 minutes. Add the coconut milk, 2 tablespoons (30 mL) maple syrup, ½ teaspoon (2.5 mL) vanilla, and the cinnamon and stir well to combine. Remove from the heat.

While the quinoa is cooking, in a small saucepan over medium-low heat, combine the strawberries, 2 tablespoons (30 mL) water, the remaining 1 tablespoon (15 mL) maple syrup, and the remaining ½ teaspoon (2.5 mL) vanilla. Cook, stirring, until the berries release their juices, about 6 minutes.

Spoon the hot quinoa into bowls. Top each bowl with 1 tablespoon (15 mL) almond butter, spoon half the warm berries over the porridge, and sprinkle each with 1 tablespoon (15 mL) almonds. Serve almond milk alongside.

PEANUT BUTTER CHIA PUDDING WITH BERRIES AND GRANOLA

SERVES 1　•　PREP TIME: 15 MINUTES OR OVERNIGHT

½ cup (125 mL) coconut creamer

1 tablespoon (15 mL) unsweetened creamy
    peanut butter

1 tablespoon (15 mL) maple syrup

3 tablespoons (45 mL) chia seeds

3 tablespoons (45 mL) unsweetened plain vegan
    yogurt, such as almond or cashew

3 tablespoons (45 mL) homemade (see page 246)
    or store-bought granola

½ cup (125 mL) berries of your choice

½ tablespoon (7.5 mL) roughly chopped
    shelled pistachios

TRUDY SAYS: For breakfast, I always want to make something nourishing and healthy, and this recipe has everything I adore. Not only is this sweet treat incredibly satisfying but it's easy to make and can even be prepared the night before.

To a blender, add the coconut creamer, 1 tablespoon (15 mL) water, the peanut butter, and maple syrup and blend until smooth.

Pour into a small bowl, add the chia seeds, and whisk until you get a puddinglike texture. Let the mixture set for 10 minutes or overnight.

Transfer to a glass and top with the yogurt, granola, berries, and pistachios.

DARK CHOCOLATE CHIP COCONUT BANANA BREAD

MAKES ONE 9-INCH LOAF; SERVES 8 TO 10
PREP TIME: 10 MINUTES • COOK TIME: 50 MINUTES

⅓ cup (80 mL) avocado oil,
   plus more for greasing the pan

2 cups (500 mL) all-purpose flour

½ cup (125 mL) coconut sugar

1½ teaspoons (7.5 mL) baking powder

1½ teaspoons (7.5 mL) baking soda

1 ripe banana

1 tablespoon (15 mL) distilled white vinegar

3.5 ounces (100 g) dark chocolate (70% cocoa),
   roughly chopped

¾ cup (180 mL) unsweetened shredded coconut

This is the perfect banana bread to whip up in your cozy kitchen on a lazy Sunday morning. It tastes 100 percent better if you make it with your pajamas on. Just saying.

Preheat the oven to 360°F (185°C) and grease a 9-by-5-inch loaf pan with oil.

Place the flour, coconut sugar, baking powder, and baking soda into a large bowl and whisk together until thoroughly combined.

In a separate medium bowl, mash the banana, then add 1½ cups (375 mL) cool water, ⅓ cup (80 mL) avocado oil, and vinegar and combine. Pour the liquid ingredients into the dry ingredients and gently stir. Add the chocolate and coconut and fold into the batter until it is smooth, with no lumps.

Pour the batter into the prepared pan and bake for 45 to 50 minutes, until a toothpick inserted into the middle comes out clean. Remove from the oven and let cool in the pan for about 1 hour.

VEGGIE TOFU SCRAMBLE

SERVES 4 TO 6 • PREP TIME: 15 MINUTES • COOK TIME: 15 MINUTES

14 ounces (396 g) firm tofu

1 tablespoon (15 mL) extra-virgin olive oil

⅓ cup (80 mL) diced red onion

2 garlic cloves, minced

1 cup (250 mL) cherry tomatoes, halved

½ cup (125 mL) diced red bell pepper

½ cup (125 mL) roughly chopped cremini mushrooms,
    stems trimmed

2 tablespoons (30 mL) unsweetened almond milk

2 teaspoons (10 mL) nutritional yeast

1 teaspoon (5 mL) ground turmeric

1 teaspoon (5 mL) freshly ground black pepper

1 teaspoon (5 mL) kosher salt

2 cups (500 mL) tightly packed fresh spinach

¼ cup (60 mL) roughly chopped fresh chives,
    for garnish (optional)

CHLOÉ WRITES: This scramble is a beloved recipe that has stood the test of time. Created more than nine years ago when I was transitioning to a plant-based diet, this savory dish has remained a brunch staple ever since. It's the perfect breakfast that is reminiscent of the typical egg scramble my mom used to make me as a child and that I adored. When I stopped eating eggs, I knew I had to re-create this traditional dish. Now I can definitely say that I never miss eggs, and this tofu scramble will forever be one of my favorite recipes.

Wrap the tofu block in a kitchen towel, place it between two sheet pans, and put a heavy weight on top, such as a cast-iron skillet or a can of beans. Press for at least 15 minutes to extract any excess liquid.

Heat the olive oil in a large frying pan over medium heat. When it starts to shimmer, add the onion and garlic and cook, stirring, until the garlic is fragrant and the onion is translucent, about 3 minutes. Add the cherry tomatoes, bell pepper, and mushrooms and cook, stirring, until the veggies start browning, about 5 minutes.

Crumble the tofu with a fork, add to the pan, and let the tofu cook, stirring occasionally, for about 3 minutes. Add the almond milk, nutritional yeast, turmeric, black pepper, and salt and stir together, evenly coating the tofu and veggies with the spices. Add the spinach and cook, stirring, until wilted, about 2 minutes.

Serve garnished with the fresh chives, if using.

SWEET POTATO WAFFLES WITH COCONUT CREAM, MAPLE SYRUP, AND BERRIES

MAKES 6 • COOK TIME: 15 MINUTES
PREP TIME: 20 MINUTES, PLUS 15 TO 30 MINUTES FOR RESTING

1 small sweet potato, peeled and cubed

1½ cups (375 mL) all-purpose flour

1 teaspoon (5 mL) baking powder

½ teaspoon (2.5 mL) pumpkin pie spice

1 flax egg: 1 tablespoon (15 mL) flaxseed meal
    stirred into 2 tablespoons (30 mL) warm water

1 cup (250 mL) unsweetened oat milk

2 tablespoons (30 mL) melted coconut oil

1 tablespoon (15 mL) maple syrup,
    plus more for serving

1 teaspoon (5 mL) vanilla extract

kosher salt

½ cup (125 mL) berries, such as blackberries,
    husk cherries, or your choice, for topping

½ cup (125 mL) unsweetened coconut cream
    or unsweetened plain vegan coconut yogurt,
    for topping

CHLOÉ WRITES: I love starting off my day with a nourishing breakfast, often opting for our yummy chia pudding or hearty quinoa porridge recipe. However, the true highlight for both my partner and me is our special breakfast on Saturday mornings. It's when we indulge in our beloved sweet potato waffles with maple syrup and berries. As we savor each bite, it's a cherished moment when the weekend unfolds and we get to spend quality time together.

Bring a small pot of water to a boil over high heat. Add the sweet potato and cook until soft when pierced with a fork or knife, about 10 minutes. Drain and mash—you should have about ½ cup (125 mL).

Sift the flour, baking powder, and pumpkin pie spice together into a medium bowl.

In another medium bowl, whisk together the mashed sweet potato, flax egg, oat milk, coconut oil, 1 tablespoon (15 mL) maple syrup, the vanilla, and a pinch of salt.

Gently fold the wet ingredients into the dry ingredients until just combined. Allow the mixture to rest 15 to 30 minutes before cooking in a waffle iron until crispy.

Serve the waffles topped with the berries, coconut cream, and maple syrup.

ASPARAGUS, PEAS, AND PESTO TART

SERVES 6 TO 8 • PREP TIME: 20 MINUTES • COOK TIME: 30 MINUTES

one 14-ounce (397 g) vegan puff pastry sheet

1 cup (250 mL) spreadable vegan cheese

1 bundle fresh asparagus,
    woody ends removed and cut in half lengthwise

1½ cups (375 mL) frozen peas

⅓ cup (80 mL) vegan pesto,
    store-bought or homemade (see page 36)

½ cup (125 mL) pickled red onions
    (see Note, page 181)

1 cup (250 mL) crumbled vegan feta

¼ cup (60 mL) roughly chopped fresh dill

⅓ cup (80 mL) roughly chopped fresh Italian parsley

⅓ cup (80 mL) roughly chopped fresh mint

1 teaspoon (5 mL) flaky sea salt

This asparagus and pea tart recipe is the best way to embrace the essence of spring. The tender asparagus spears and plump peas come together on a vegan buttery crust, creating a harmonious blend of flavors. Inspired by the fresh produce at our local market, this tart captures the heart of the season perfectly. With each bite, you'll experience the vibrant taste of spring in a truly delicious way.

Remove the pastry sheet from the freezer and thaw in the fridge 1 hour prior to baking.

Preheat the oven to 400°F (200°C) and line a baking pan with parchment paper.

Unfold the pastry sheet and place lengthwise on the prepared baking pan.

Spread the vegan cheese to cover the pastry sheet, leaving a ½-inch border around the edge. Add the asparagus lengthwise, then disperse the peas evenly over the top. Drizzle with the pesto from left to right.

Bake for 25 to 30 minutes, or until the crust is golden. Remove from the oven and let cool for 5 minutes. Top with the pickled onions, vegan feta, dill, parsley, and mint and sprinkle with the sea salt.

SAVORY CHICKPEA PANCAKES

MAKES 8 TO 10 • PREP TIME: 20 MINUTES • COOK TIME: 15 MINUTES

2 cups (500 mL) chickpea flour

2 tablespoons (30 mL) nutritional yeast

1 teaspoon (5 mL) baking powder

1 teaspoon (5 mL) garlic powder

1 teaspoon (5 mL) ground sumac

kosher salt and freshly ground black pepper

¾ cup (180 mL) grated zucchini

1½ cups (375 mL) roughly chopped bell peppers

¾ cup (180 mL) peeled and grated carrots

⅓ cup (80 mL) roughly chopped shallot

1 tablespoon (15 mL) apple cider vinegar

6 tablespoons (90 mL) extra-virgin olive oil, divided

8 cherry tomatoes, halved, for topping

3 scallions, sliced, for topping

1 cup (250 mL) broccoli sprouts, for topping

FOR THE SPREAD

2 tablespoons (30 mL) vegan pesto,
    store-bought or homemade (see page 36)

3 tablespoons (45 mL) tahini

3 tablespoons (45 mL) freshly squeezed lemon juice

1 teaspoon (5 mL) red wine vinegar

Your breakfast routine might change after you've had these. They are so irresistibly savory that you'll find yourself craving breakfast for dinner and vice versa. Whether you're seeking a healthy brunch or a cozy dinner, these chickpea pancakes will leave you feeling satisfied and nourished. This protein-rich comfort food proves that indulging in pancakes does not only need to be a morning affair.

Preheat the oven to 175°F (80°C).

In a large bowl, mix together the chickpea flour, nutritional yeast, baking powder, garlic powder, and sumac, and season with salt and pepper.

Place the grated zucchini on a kitchen towel and squeeze out any excess moisture. Combine the zucchini, bell peppers, carrots, and shallot in a large bowl and set aside.

In another large bowl, whisk together 1¼ cups (310 mL) water, the apple cider vinegar, and 2 tablespoons (30 mL) olive oil until the mixture is emulsified. Pour the wet ingredients into the dry ingredients and stir to combine to a smooth pancake batter.

Add the vegetable mixture to the pancake batter and mix until well combined.

Heat 2 tablespoons (30 mL) olive oil in a medium skillet or non-stick pan over medium-low heat. When it starts to shimmer, add ½ cup (125 mL) of the pancake mixture to the skillet. Beware: chickpea flour heats up very quickly and can burn easily, so make sure to keep an eye on the pancake. Cook on one side for 45 seconds, flip, and cook on the other side for another 45 seconds. Place the pancake on an oven-safe plate in the oven to keep warm. Repeat with the remaining batter, adding more olive oil as needed. ➤➤

◄◄ *Make the spread:* In a small bowl, whisk together the vegan pesto, tahini, and lemon juice. Once combined, add the red wine vinegar and 1 tablespoon (15 mL) water and combine. The spread should have a smooth texture.

Serve the pancakes topped with the spread, cherry tomatoes, scallions, and sprouts.

INDEX

CHLOÉ CRANE-LEROUX is a recipe developer, creative director, and food photographer. Her work has been featured in renowned publications such as the *New York Times*, *Forbes*, and more. Originally from Montreal, Chloé pursued her studies at the prestigious Parsons School of Design in New York City with a BFA in photography. Her creativity extends to engaging videos and captivating visuals, earning her collaborations with luxury brands like Chanel and Dior and lifestyle brands such as J.Crew and Anthropologie. Chloé's passion for plant-based cuisine invites people to savor nature's bounty while making eco-conscious choices. Her culinary artistry elevates plant-based cooking, making each meal an artistic experience. She lives in New York City.

TRUDY CRANE is a ceramic artist who has established herself under the brand name lookslikewhite, a reflection of her minimalist aesthetic, which has been featured in publications such as *House & Home*, *House Beautiful*, *Martha Stewart Weddings*, and many others. She has also worked collaboratively with companies like Food52, creating bespoke collections that add a touch of artisanal craftsmanship to the culinary world. Beyond her ceramics, Trudy is an active mature model. She promotes diversity and encourages a pro-age attitude in an industry often preoccupied with youth. In addition to her creative pursuits, Trudy extends her passion for a conscious lifestyle to her role as a vegan cookbook author. Together, Trudy and her daughter, Chloé Crane-Leroux, craft recipes that not only delight the taste buds but also speak to the beauty of the table and the world around us. She lives in Montreal, Canada.